MAKING AND BREAKING FAMILIES

MAKING AND BREAKING FAMILIES

The way ahead for parents and their children

Jill Curtis

FREE ASSOCIATION BOOKS / LONDON / NEW YORK

Published in 1998 by
FREE ASSOCIATION BOOKS
57 Warren Street, London W1P 5PA
and 70 Washington Square South,
New York, NY 10012–1091

© Jill Curtis 1998 *T32664 306.850941 CUR*

The right of Jill Curtis to be identified as the author
of this work has been asserted by her in accordance
with the Copyright, Designs and Patents Act 1988.

A CIP catalogue record for this book is available
from the British Library

ISBN 1 85343 411 6 hbk; 1 85343 412 4 pbk

Designed, typeset and produced for Free Association Books by
Chase Production Services, Chadlington, OX7 3LN
Printed in the EC by J.W. Arrowsmith Ltd, Bristol

FOR JESSICA, HANNAH AND JOSHUA

The sweetest of all enjoyments which God has sent us [is] a taste for domestic pleasures. Those which are sought for far from home are trouble and weariness of mind, and weakness and pain of body; on the contrary, the felicity which is enjoyed in the bosom of our families is always within our reach, and healthful both to the mind and body. Without domestic happiness, no other joys are able to procure us lasting satisfaction, or tranquillity, but when this is secure, all others please.

MARY WOLLSTONECRAFT
'Introductory Address to Parents' in the
Elements of Morality for the Use of Children, 1792

Contents

Acknowledgements

I COULD NOT HAVE written this book without the help of the men, women and children who were generous enough to share with me their experiences of family life. I am grateful to them for the frank way they were prepared to discuss situations which were often very painful for them.

It made me realise and appreciate how fortunate I am to be surrounded by the warmth of a loving family who all contribute daily to my understanding and views about family life.

My daughter, Virginia, the co-author of *Where's Daddy?*, my previous book on divorce, gave me much of her time and help with the research for this one, as did my husband, John, who supported me with his love and patience and gave freely of his invaluable editorial expertise in guiding this book to fruition. I want also to thank my mother for her advice and encouragement.

My friend David Gentleman has enhanced the appearance of the book by his handsome and appropriate drawing for the cover of the paperback edition.

Linda Farley, the librarian of the British Association of Psychotherapists, was always helpful, knowledgeable and efficient.

Preface

WHETHER YOU ARE a professional working with families or a parent trying to understand your own domestic situation, the structure of many families today will be different from that of the family you grew up in.

There is no longer a simple way to recognize the composition of a family. Tremendous changes in the patterns of family life have taken place in the second half of the twentieth century. The status of marriage and the structure of the family altered and developed as society evolved over the years, but with nothing like the speed and upheaval experienced in recent times. There was no judicial divorce in England before the Matrimonial Causes Act in 1857, which then dominated the divorce law until the reforms of the Divorce Reform Act in 1969. This brought about a major change, away from divorce based on matrimonial offence to divorce grounded on irretrievable breakdown of the marriage. Another big change is on the horizon with the Family Law Act due to be implemented in 1999. The emphasis is that the parties should not look *backwards*, fastening on the blame and guilt of one of the partners, but before taking the irretrievable step of divorce they should, with professional help, plan and look *towards the future*.

Better healthcare means that people live longer, and marriages may last forty, fifty and even sixty years. The rise of feminism, hand in hand with effective birth control, has altered our perception of a woman's place in the home. These are examples of the changes which have played their part in bringing about shifts which would have been inconceivable in our grandparents' lifetimes.

This book looks at how the selection of a partner is determined by unconscious as well as conscious decisions, how our own early experiences influence our ability to form lasting relationships and why it is that while some families survive, others fall at the first fence. The 'family' must now be seen in various different guises. No longer can it be assumed that a couple marry, have children and live happily ever after. England is the divorce capital of Europe, and two in three marriages fail. And after the separation, where do the children fit in? Society may no longer frown upon divorce, but it has taken more time to wake up to the problems caused by the splitting and merging which inevitably follow, and of the effect upon the children. This erosion of traditional family values affects everyone, not just those involved in particular cases, but society at large.

In one week in January 1998 *The Times* reported details of a twelve-year-old becoming the youngest father in Britain, and of a sixty-three-year-old woman becoming a mother after fertility treatment. What does this tell us, and what is more important tell our children, about the importance of commitment and relationships, and responsibility towards others?

The family unit is the bedrock of society. But the balance within the family group is shifting and we must be prepared for the change. As families split up and regroup, new compositions become established. Many families are now supported by lone parents, particularly mothers. In addition to stepfamilies, my research highlighted several other kinds of family grouping. Blended families where second partners and children have divided loyalties are all too common. There is a fast-growing number of families where the grandparents have become parents of their children's children. There are families where one, or both parents, are gay or lesbian, with custody of a child or children from a previous relationship. A recognized group of married couples has banded together to be acknowledged as 'non parents'. There are even 'double families' where a father shares his time between two families, who are sometimes not even aware of the other's existence. The chorus of family experiences is fortunately also joined by couples who have been happily married for almost a lifetime.

These different family structures require professionals working with families to have an understanding and knowledge of what these changes imply. They need to be fully aware of all the complexities involved as they encounter adults and children faced with the problems of regrouping as a family, and all too often coping at the same time with prejudices directed at families which are seen to be 'different'. Is it right that the 'family' still has to be the one so admired in the 1960s, the nuclear family? For the combination of a man and woman usually married with two or three children is no longer representative of the norm in society. Is this change necessarily catastrophic? Or is it because the shift from the familiar makeup of a family to alternative and often previously unacknowledged patterns makes us anxious? How acceptable are these alternatives? Some more than others maybe, and are they sufficient to keep the fabric of society intact? How important are our own experiences of early family relationships when we, in turn, choose a partner and create our own family?

As social workers, counsellors and therapists know, the old template of family life can be idealized and those in the helping professions are continually confronted by adults and children who are struggling to free themselves from unhealthy family tangles. Nevertheless, on the plus side, a traditional family, a network of caring people, does provide a sense of security and a feeling of belonging, especially for the children and the elderly.

These are the issues and questions which are addressed in this book. The concept of the family is changing, so a search for new formulas is inevitable. We should be prepared to accept that other groupings can provide the emotional warmth and the caring attention to material needs which are so necessary for mental and physical well-being.

As in my previous book *Where's Daddy?* the men, women and children speak for themselves, although all names have been changed to observe confidentiality. They pose questions and search for answers. Some believe they have found solutions and their experiences will pave the way for others in similar situations. The voices of some professionals working with adults and children and families are heard as well. So too are those who have experienced a lifetime of contentment from their marriages. Hopefully what they all have contributed will help others to take a fresh and unprejudiced look at the structure of the family at the end of the twentieth century.

Jill Curtis
London, 1998

1   The Role of the Family

> All happy families resemble one another. Each unhappy family is
> unhappy in its own way.
>
> Leo Tolstoy, War and Peace

The Family and Marriage

Traditionally the family provides a secure setting for its members. One
of its functions is to protect the young and to prepare them for the
outside world, the larger 'family' we all have to face. The family also
provides a child with patterns of behaviour to use as standards for life
in society at large; and, of course, the guidelines for creating, in time,
his or her own family.

Freud was the first to show the crucial importance of infantile
experience in the development of the personality and its disorders. Of
particular relevance in today's divorce-ridden society, is the way he
linked anxiety resulting from loss of the person a child loves, with
neurotic anxiety in later life.

Since Freud we have been inundated with evidence which stresses the
importance of those first family attachments if relationships are to be
maintained in adult life. Harlow's work is well documented: the results
of his experiments with monkeys and his study of the long-term effects of
separating young monkeys from their mothers are familiar and impres-
sive (Harlow, 1959). Dr John Bowlby's ground-breaking work on the
importance of the early relationships of infants and the part they subsequently play in adult mental health has had far-reaching influence on the
care of children. His evidence that separation from the mother can be
traumatic for the child is conclusive (Bowlby, 1969 and 1973). All the
growing mass of knowledge goes to show that the presence or absence of
the mother is of paramount importance in determining the child's emotional state and has had a profound effect on the way infants and children
are cared for.

D.W. Winnicott, the paediatrician, child psychiatrist and psychoanalyst, introduced the term 'good enough mothering' to describe the
ups and downs in normal mother/child interaction, and this helped to
dismiss the idea that only a perfect or ideal mother would do. In his paper
'Primary Maternal Preoccupation' (1956) he outlines the way a mother
gradually identifies with her infant, and the value of this early period

both for mother and baby. Until his influence began to be felt, recognition of the overriding importance of the mother/child relationship had the effect of neglecting the significance of the father. It was through the work of Winnicott that the importance of the family as a unit was appreciated, encompassing such ideas as that the father's practical and emotional support of the mother enabled her to be free of anxieties and to turn her attention to the care of her baby (Winnicott, 1960). Winnicott gave a series of radio talks in 1944 and one of the questions he posed was, 'What About Father?', a paper subsequently included in *The Child, the Family and the Outside World* (1964). He believed it is not always a good idea to put the baby to bed before the father comes home. In fact, 'it is a great help in the relation between married people when they share day by day the little details of experience in the care of their infant'. This important time allows for the bond between the child and parents to become even stronger. He emphasizes once again that the father is valuable in helping the mother to feel happy 'in her body and mind' and in backing her authority. The father is also needed to enrich the child's world, both by his personality and by contributing his outside experiences. Most important of all, according to Winnicott, what a father does for his children is to be alive and to stay alive during the child's early years. This was, of course, written before the large cloud of divorce spread over so many families with young children, and left them either without a father or with a part-time one.

James Robertson recorded the adverse effects on children who were separated from their mothers when in hospital (Robertson, 1958). The film 'Going to Hospital with Mother' made a great impression on the mothers of the 1960s. And, following this evidence, there has been a significant change in recent years in the care of children in hospital; it is now accepted that the family has a major role to contribute in the recovery of a son or daughter, and the parents are encouraged to stay with the child and to play a large part in the nursing.

Psychoanalytic psychotherapist Josephine Klein, in *Our Need for Others* (1987), drawing upon material from psychoanalytic writers such as Balint, Tustin, Guntrip and of course Bowlby and Winnicott, gives a full and clear account of the way in which the first few months of life affect our future relationships. Klein provides a searching overview of the increased recognition of our need for others from infancy onwards, the time when either a secure or insecure foundation is laid for the development of personality structure. She asks the question, 'What of children who do not have these early good experiences?' Her answer is, 'early insufficiencies can leave structural weakness which leads people to experience themselves as fragmented, liable to fall apart, not really alive, only *pretending to be people* [my italics]. They need holding before they are healed. They need a considerable period of very secure attachment.'

For someone who has not had this rewarding early experience, yet craves to be held, a romantic 'falling in love' can bring about the blissful feeling of secure attachment:

JANICE: *'I always felt scared and out of things as a child. I met Billy and fell for him right away. He made me feel good. I knew I wanted to marry him, and we got married six months later. What went wrong was when he wanted to be with his friends – I couldn't see why we couldn't be together all the time. That was what I thought marriage would be. I can see now I was impossible. We had a baby, but that didn't help, made it worse.'*

Janice describes the desperate need to belong to somebody in order to feel safe. With Billy, in marriage, she thought she had found just that. The opposite happened and when Billy wanted to have time with his friends Janice felt as bereft as she had as a baby when left by her mother. Neither Billy nor Janice could understand her powerful reactions which were seen by both as unreasonable behaviour.

JANICE: *'He went off with a friend of mine – said he couldn't stand my moods and jealousy.'*

Modern research has also concentrated on family grouping and has revealed just how complicated relationships can be, how choice of a partner is based both on conscious and unconscious decisions. Dr Peter Cook's work has been concerned with primary prevention in child and family mental health in many different countries. In his book *Early Child Care – Infants and Nations at Risk* (1996) he says, 'During the first three years the foundations of the love life are being laid, both for the child and the future adult. It follows *that preparation for marriage begins at birth.* So does preparation for being a lover and a parent.'

On the conscious level it is often easy to say why one 'falls in love', what it is we find attractive about the other, but the decision will most often be based on an instinctive feeling that the other person will truly understand and meet our deepest needs. However, with the unconscious playing its part, elements and traces of our early experiences of close relationships will have been recognized. Years into marriage many couples are surprised by the way they thought they had married a partner very different from a parent, only to find the opposite. With the unconscious at work familiar traits from the past will surface. A close intimate adult partnership will awake memories of both good and bad experiences of early childhood.

Stella Dick, a psychotherapist engaged in marital and family work spoke from her own experience as a practitioner:

> STELLA: *'I find that a crucial element in this is the search for the illusory other half – "illusory" because two halves make a "one" not a couple. Where this is not understood and dealt with, the couple or family unit remains fragile in the face of life's stresses and many do not survive them. What feels to be a crisis in the partnership can offer up opportunities for new possibilities.'*

Dick believes that we impose our own expectations upon the other, creating in him or her the image of our own glamorous ideal and then ourselves falling under the magic of the spell we have created. If the spell is broken, we are left with the partner who lacks our idealized qualities and major readjustment must be made. As Dick pointed out, this can be a time for creating a new, truthful relationship. Too often, though, it is a time for flight.

In the twentieth century when people are no longer constrained by their immediate environment, selection of a partner from the global village is no easy step. And just as we have benefited from understanding more about the dynamics which make or break a family, so there is a plethora of advice on forming and maintaining relationships. The result is that expectations are higher, but tolerance is lower. Greater psychological analysis has made people expect relationships of a higher calibre. Giving thought to the quality of the relationship and trying to understand the psychological impact a couple have upon each other ought to mean a better marriage. But as today there is a greater emphasis on individualization, so it seems it is harder to find lasting satisfaction in a relationship.

No longer are such diagnoses confined to professional marital and family therapists and counsellors. Every woman's magazine has advice about 'listening to your partner' or a questionnaire on 'how to tell if you are both still in love'. Discussions about sexual issues and fulfilment are commonplace, and all this does often have a serious impact on the family: no longer is 'making your bed and lying on it' an adage that is upheld. Certainly, sexual incompatibility is often given as a reason for marital breakdown.

Consider the influence and appeal of Skynner and Cleese when they collaborated to write *Families and How to Survive Them* (1983). Apart from the charismatic appeal of the authors, this guide to family survival was popular because Skynner and Cleese had the ability to pinpoint areas of family strife and to give guidelines for handling the situation. Written in plain language it is about situations recognizable to most lay readers who were somewhat comforted by identifying similar conflicts within their own families. Within my own psychotherapeutic practice I heard from many patients how after reading this guide they had begun to look at their own family dynamics, perhaps for the first time, and to question how this had influenced the way they think and behave. Often the next step had then been to seek psychotherapy for themselves.

The arrival of a third person, a child, into the relationship of a couple brings about a shift in the dynamics – in other words can alter the delicate balance of the conscious and unconscious expectations which were the reasons for the relationship to have taken root in the first place.

JULIE: *'Jack and I were happy together. What we couldn't deal with was having a baby. Jack had never wanted to be a father.'*

Through his work as a marital and family therapist Skynner has also made considerable major contributions to understanding the importance of the father in a family. In his book *Family Matters* (1995) he recalls that when he first worked in a child guidance clinic in the 1950s fathers had 'yet to be discovered'. Taking his lead from pioneering work in the USA Skynner began to include fathers in work with families with great success. Today this is an accepted practice, and fathers, who it was wrongly assumed would be reluctant, will accept an invitation to be part of therapy sessions.

As children we become aware of who we are through our relationships with those around us, and when these relationships break down the effect is long lasting and, in turn, affects society. There were 173,510 divorces in 1995 and 86,000 of those were with couples with children under sixteen years of age, bringing the colossal total number of children in these broken families to 160,563 (Office for National Statistics). In addition 'adult' children too, are deeply affected by their parents' divorce. These figures are not recorded. The charity Families Need Fathers found that in the previous year 50 per cent of married fathers from these broken families lost all contact with their children after three years. How can so many children *not* have been affected by the marital strife? Frequently this causes the onset of symptoms in the child such as bed-wetting, tearfulness, withdrawal or behavioural problems which may signal that something is wrong with the family dynamic. The time leading up to a separation can be an especially disruptive and bewildering one for a child. Children can, and do, notice changes in their parents' relationship, and a child's physical or emotional complaints may appear long before it is acknowledged there is trouble between the mother and father. Children are very tuned in to the adults' inner turmoil, often – with hindsight – to the astonishment of the parents. The parents may be devastated or relieved by divorce, the children can be left frightened and confused.

The End of a Marriage

With one in two marriages breaking down families have now to be restructured in a variety of ways. There are those parents who on finding that they have become one-parent families go it alone. With those who remarry the possibility of a subsequent divorce is high. So although families may blend and merge the shadow of a further split must not be discounted.

Judith Wallerstein in her highly acclaimed study known as the 'California Children of Divorce Project', and her subsequent work, made us very much aware that 'children of divorce' do suffer and go on suffering. She also discovered that half the children she assessed saw one parent get a second divorce within a decade of the first. Wallerstein's work is ongoing and is much valued. *Surviving the Breakup* by Wallerstein and Kelly (1980) is still a work of great importance in the understanding of the effects on children after divorce. It was her early work which drew attention to a serious malaise of our time and altered forever our view of the short- and long-term effects of a family breakdown.

As we hear in later chapters, those who feel they have made a fresh start after the breakup of their first family, find only too often that the same difficulties emerge the second time around – especially if there is no real understanding about what went wrong the first time, and what caused the separation.

> ANNA: *'I was seven when my dad left us, and nine when mum remarried. I never liked Ron and was glad to see him go a year later. Of course, as an adult, now I feel very sad about what happened to us as a family. My most vivid memories are of my mother in tears.'*

The breakdown of a family, for whatever reason, causes untold grief to all concerned, not only to the immediate family unit, but to all the relatives in the extended family as well. Indeed, the impact spreads wider than this, and often close friends and their children feel the painful knock-on effect just as powerfully as relatives do.

Even if both partners are in agreement that a separation is the only possible course of action, there is sadness at the failure of it all. The buildup prior to the irrevocable decision is frequently a time of quarrels and suffering, often with physical and psychological ill-health affecting both parents and the children.

LAURIE: *'I knew I couldn't go on living with my then wife. We were at each other's throats day and night, and that certainly didn't help us or the kids. The time we decided to call it a day was the saddest in my life. The relief I felt soon merged into misery as I realized the full impact of the decision we had just made.'*

The decision to separate, made jointly or unilaterally, is one which has lasting repercussions for all concerned and should never be made lightly. At one time – not so very long ago – marriage was seen as a solemn lifelong contract between a couple. One of the primary purposes of the legal bond of marriage was for the rearing and protection of children. In the last twenty years the number of lone-parent families has grown from 8.6 per cent to 22 per cent of all families.

These statistics showing the rise in the number of divorces is a misleading understatement: the figures do not include the unmarried couples who break up. We need to include those couples who do not marry, yet have a child and live together with commitment, and then whose partnership fails. Almost two million children in Britain live in broken homes (*European Union Survey*, 1996), which is *twice* the European average. And divorce is now increasing even in countries where religious and legal impediments to it are still strong. Divorce became legal in Ireland in 1997 for couples who have lived apart for four years: about 90,000 people are believed to be separated, of whom a quarter is now expected to start divorce proceedings.

The proliferation of so many broken homes has had a calamitous impact on the children of the families concerned. How to attack this problem is one of the themes of this book. The number of couples who seriously contemplate separation, but then decide their difficulties can be resolved, cannot of course be recorded. But unfortunately, the focus must be on the large percentage of the population now faced by the trauma of divorce and its aftermath. They are left with the pain of a failed partnership which can have a further damaging effect on future intimate relationships.

MARIE: *'I have been divorced for eight years. I meet men of all ages and from all kinds of different circumstances and walks of life. Many are great guys – yet I'm not prepared to share all my time, feelings or my life with them. I am still not ready to put my past marriage behind me or to forget the hurt I've been through. My ex is now on to his third marriage (including ours) and has a little boy too. He seems to have put the past well and truly behind him.'*

It is hard to regain a sense of trust after a broken marriage has torn a family apart and this feeling of unease can cast a cloud over subsequent relationships, and a nagging anxiety about how to set out to create a new or blended family. Don is still bewildered about why his marriage failed. He told us he was truly puzzled about what the modern woman thinks marriage is for. It seemed to him that providing a safe platform for bringing up children no longer seems to fit the equation.

DON: *'The prevailing thought seems to be "if it doesn't work out, get out" with the justification that it is better to bring up a child without a father than in a "bad" marriage. I lost a wife and kids and I really don't know why.'*

JIM: *'Whatever happened to self-discipline, commitment, dedication, selflessness and duty? That's what keeps a marriage strong and couples together.'*

On hearing Jim's comments, Ruth wanted her contribution to be put next to Jim's:

RUTH: *'What happened to commitment and duty? I can answer that. They went out of the window when my husband beat the tar out of me on a regular basis.'*

Reasons Marriages Break Down

There is no single cause for broken relationships. For some, the flight *into* marriage is a desire for closeness, companionship and security. The shattered dreams which result if these do not materialize may bring about a collapse of the partnership. Marital failure is the breakdown of human relationships. To achieve the position of equality in a marriage – a true partnership – it requires personalities who are able to adapt, be flexible and stable, and to negotiate with each other without negation or destruction.

Psychoanalytic psychotherapist Stanley Ruszczynski who works clinically with individuals and couples, sums up what he considers to be the healthy characteristics needed by a couple in a psychologically sound relationship: 'a sense of psychological separateness as well as commitment to the relationship, is one of them' (Ruszczynski, 1992). If this position is not reached there will be difficulties in communication, and frustration and a grudge about the loss of independence, or of self.

SUSAN: *'I used to be a pretty bright spark – I think that is why Kevin married me. Two years into marriage I couldn't tell where he ended and I began. I started all my sentences with "Kevin says", "Kevin feels". I quite simply felt lost. When I met Jack, I began to think and speak for myself and realized that Kevin and I had merged in a very unhealthy way. Kevin never could understand why I left him, and I couldn't explain it really.'*

SALLY: *'When I was settled in my job after college I thought, great, that's the first part, now its time to get married and that's just what I did. I thought it would make my world complete. Unfortunately the reality was I hadn't taken into account the fact marriage is a contract of people not just a life plan. Now I am divorced. I am only thankful we hadn't had a child.'*

JUDE: *'This may sound naive but I didn't think about working at my marriage and I realize when my then husband upset me I used to react in a very childish "temper tantrum" way. I used to behave like that with my parents when I was a girl and just went on doing it. It never occurred to me to get a grip and face up to the problem. For me it was tears or silence and I truly regret that. I believe I killed off the love we had at the start.'*

We heard from many couples who felt they had married before their growing-up process had been completed. Within a framework of marriage, some couples can allow for this, while for others resentment and jealousy cloud the situation when one or the other is felt to be left behind, either emotionally or intellectually. For some couples the marriage may not initially have been a mistake, but the parties grew apart. They may have developed in different directions. Quite possibly, it would have been very hard to anticipate or predict this, although research in America is attempting to study long-term relationships, in the hope of identifying signals which predict the future breakdown of a partnership. John Gottman, Professor of Psychology at the University of Washington, has developed a 'repair and maintenance' programme for couples in his Seattle 'Love Lab'. He also studies couples who stay happily married and he found that contrary to myth 'it was not financial ease or compatibility that made the difference, but the way happy couples steered their way through disagreements without drowning in the destructive rapids of criticism, contempt, defensiveness and silent sulks'. To understand more about the ways that couples can find the 'magic' – as Professor Gottman calls it – he combined the application of science with the art of love. His findings could perhaps be beneficial if only to help lessen the feelings of guilt or failure after a marriage collapses. It could help reduce the tension and resentment which can provide such an unhealthy atmosphere both for the children and adults to absorb. When the parents embroil the children in their problems, either consciously or unconsciously, the children continue to suffer.

Parents sometimes decide to stay together 'for the sake of the children'. However, although this may be the reason on the surface, there are often deeper causes like fear of being on one's own, fear of family disapproval, or even fear of the unknown. The children can become a handy excuse, but this in turn puts an unbearable pressure on them.

A healthy balanced marriage can only survive if underpinned in a positive way. It cannot flourish under pressures such as infidelity, violence, unreliability, chemical or physical abuse. However, some marriages can and do continue with these pressures or with others, such as with one partner or child suffering from a severe physical or mental disorder. Not enough research has been carried out to ascertain why some couples can hold together in adversity whilst others fall at the first or second fences. One cause may well be that not enough couples are prepared for the hard work that must go into any marriage if it is to survive over the years.

The present climate contributes greatly to the increase in marriages breaking up. If marriage is not seen as a lifelong commitment - and the transitory nature of marriage is how it is portrayed in the media, in films, in novels, etc. – the door is left ajar, and then one or other partner will leave through it. The message given out today is a mixed and often confusing one: it is to be hoped we teach that love should go hand in hand with commitment and responsibility.

We allow young people to be bombarded by sexual images and entice them with a 'go for it, don't worry about relationships' attitude. The contraceptive pill brought about sexual freedom for women; we now hear of women talking about 'recreational sex' at the same time as society's attitude to abortion has become more relaxed. But have these, and similar changes of attitude, combined to give a message that there is no price to be paid? That there is, after all, such a thing as a free lunch? In later chapters we hear from men, women and children who have paid a high price as a result.

Throw away plastic containers, at a pinch recycle your paper and bottles, but somewhere along the line we have lost sight of the strengths that a tight-knit family can provide. If one family – or car – doesn't please, trade it in for another! Is this truly the message we want to pass on to the next generation?

This is a problem spreading across the world. From one man in Bombay we heard of a growing anxiety in India. Sunil told us that for him, 'Divorce is not an option', but he said that the fear was being widely expressed that this 'fashion' might find its way to India as other Western beliefs have done. Others in India contacted us on the Internet, with the same message: 'In marriage one must learn to live together.' 'Both the man and woman must mould in a way that they can live and love together.' 'They learn to live in a way to protect the children.' We asked, what if this doesn't happen? 'But it just *does*,' came back reply after reply. Some puzzlement was expressed when we questioned further: 'It is expected', we were told. In Japan divorce is still rare and almost all marriages are first marriages; one quarter of current marriages were described as 'arranged' rather than love matches.

Brian in Hong Kong felt that in the Western world we had all become blinkered by the escape route of divorce. This sounded positive to us, until he continued:

BRIAN: '*Women here will protect the family by turning a blind eye to the extramarital needs of their husbands. A mistress is expected – and does not threaten the family life in any way.*'

SONG joined in: '*When I go to England on business my wife does my packing, and although we never speak of it, she always packs a supply of condoms for me.*'

Woefully one woman commented:

NAZEEN: '*Yes, an Asian wife will comply – but don't let her imagine that a woman could behave in that way. It would be the end of the family, and the wife has responsibility for that.*'

INGA in Germany: '*We do not have as many divorces as you in Britain, but we are aware of the numbers of children affected by divorce here. We have a word "Scheidungswaisen" which means "divorce orphan". A sad word.*'

But to return to the attitude in Britain:

> BILL: *'My parents drifted through a very dull marriage. God knows if they were happy. I was married to Anne for five years, and once my marriage reached the doldrums I left. Life is for living!'*

Yes, indeed, life is for living. But what are these doldrums Bill is describing? Looking at his own family history helps us to understand that Bill was never encouraged by his parents to discuss and to talk through a difficult situation. Unhappy families do not teach their children how to manage pain and when Bill's marriage hit a rough spot he was off. Like drugs or alcohol, getting a divorce is a mistaken way of avoiding pain.

The explosive conflicts do not bring about the breakup of a family, and they often release the tension. A major cause can be the inability of the members of the family to deal with these tensions within the group and to clear them up without rejection or scapegoating one another. To many practitioners it is an all too familiar story to hear of one way of putting an end to problems within the family, when they are told of the father leaving the family behind. Frequently the solution appears to be to avoid pain *at that moment* almost at any price. The pain that is waiting around the corner, and this includes anguish for the children, has to be met head-on eventually when the full sorrow of the separation is felt.

Revenge and feelings of resentment, often hidden even from oneself, are the chief stumbling blocks which can spoil relationships. Counsellors and therapists are continually faced, when working with clients or patients, with the task of bringing these resentments into conscious thought and then confronting them. No one can make deep personal relationships if feelings are blocked by bitterness filling the unconscious. These grudges can be projected onto partners and the therapist can find the session time filled with complaints of 'he will never ...' or 'she doesn't ...'. It is not easy for a couple at war to accept that what has happened has been contributed to by both – the result of their combined failure to create a proper relationship as a couple. Revenge is strongest when feeling that the magic cast at the beginning of a relationship has vanished into thin air. Even then, magic is often expected from the therapist, to provide a solution and a quick fix.

The man looking to his new wife for continual mothering, or the woman who fears she will find in her partner the rejection she felt from her father, is already setting out in a leaky boat on the sea of matrimony. Likewise, the much loved daughter may seek in a husband – quite unconsciously – the uncritical love of a devoted parent and consequently the transition to wife and partner can be a painful one. For some, the gulf is too wide to bridge and the search for a new 'ideal' and 'understanding' partner continues. The old trick of saying 'my wife/husband doesn't understand me' is all about the wife or husband understanding only too well, and at the same time not fulfilling the expected projections of the spouse. Romantic love as portrayed in films and novels is a poor template for marriage. It taps into the hope that there is a someone who will satisfy our every wish unconditionally.

When a newlywed discovers that his or her beloved has a previously unacknowledged personality and identity of his or her own, the honeymoon is truly over. If there has been no earlier experience within the childhood family of how to settle disagreements, to balance cooperation with individualization, to appreciate honesty and sincerity and to develop a true concern for others, then an adult relationship can well flounder.

Qualities and values of this kind are not really taught, but are absorbed as we grow up from the adults around us. If a child is brought up in a family where instant gratification is the norm – if one relationship isn't working then swap it for another – that too will have been absorbed into the formation of the character of the child.

Even with good intentions on the part of both parents there are situations which can bring about the breakdown of a family. A study by the Joseph Rowntree Foundation pinpointed the stress on family life when one out of every four fathers works more than fifty hours a week. This severely restricts the time each father can spend with his family. Moreover, the mothers are more likely to suffer from ill effects as well, such as depression, and thus a great strain is put on the marriage and family.

GEORGE: *'I was on the road and away from home most of the week. Our family did suffer. I was too tired when I was at home to notice. I wasn't really surprised when my wife found somebody else. We hadn't been a couple for a long time.'*

George pinpoints one essential element in building and keeping a family – it takes time and energy and George had neither to offer his family.

SUE: *'We split up – no one else was involved for either of us, but once Jim was made redundant the grind of it all tore us to bits. I went home to live with my mum and took Kevin with me. Sad, really.'*

What really went wrong here? Obviously, external circumstances brought enormous pressures to bear on this family – but there are families who would have clung together in the storm and had inner resources which could have been tapped to keep them afloat. Kevin, aged seven, lost so much that year and the opportunity to see his parents' marriage survive, against all odds, was only one of them.

The crisis in schools is linked to troubled families. The media is swift to point a finger at single-parent families and at absent middle-class fathers and blame them for the growing ranks of expelled pupils. Research by OFSTED (Office for Standards in Education) showed that the majority of those involved had absent fathers either through a work commitment or marital breakdown. The Headmasters and Headmistresses' Conference spoke out in 1996 about the danger to classroom order posed by parents too busy to care for their children. The chairman of the conference called for a national debate to discuss the situation: that schools are having to cope with the emotional crises of children whose parents were unavailable, either because of a separation, or because they were too busy to talk to them.

The Relationship Revolution

The phrase 'The Relationship Revolution' has been coined by Duncan J. Dormor in his book with that title (1992). This comprehensive study of marriage and partnerships was carried out by One plus One, an organization which was founded in 1971 to increase understanding about contemporary marriage, and to put research into practice for the prevention of marital breakdown. The report considers the 1950s, which was the heyday of what we now call the traditional family with 'the emphasis on fulfilling the roles of husband and wife, mother and father, rather than the pursuit of personal happiness'. Once more the emphasis is on the shift which has occurred in marriage in the post-Second-World-War period. In 1945 the UK was – for the first time, but by no means the last – confronted by the effects of a tidal wave of divorces sweeping the country. It is a sobering thought that the children of these families brought up during the war became, in time, the parents in the 1960s. The effect that lengthy separations and wartime stress had on all children is difficult to establish, but only too easy to appreciate. Winnicott was deeply involved with the care of children who were evacuated during the war. So, too, was James Robertson, who was later responsible for making us look at the care of children in hospital in such a different light. Ilse Helman, in her book *From War Babies to Grandmothers* (1990), describes her observations at the Hampstead War Nurseries where she had ample opportunity to study the effect of separation upon young children. The evacuation of children from cities was designed to save them from physical harm. It was only later that the emotional harm resulting from the separation from their mothers and homes was recognized.

On the return of husbands from the war many couples found themselves virtual strangers. Children were 'introduced' to their fathers and the men themselves often found it hard to establish their position with the mother and child. The pressure on families was enormous and the situation was often compounded by the arrival of a new baby.

JIM: *'When I came home I didn't know my five-year-old daughter. We had a baby a year later, and then I felt we were a family.'*

DENISE: *'Joe and I married far too quickly. Marry in haste as they say. When he came back from the war four years later we began married life. It was like living with a stranger. We were very unhappy, but we managed – divorce wasn't even thought about.'*

Denise and Joe did not have long enough to build a relationship; to marry quickly because of the threat of separation and possible death prevented them from becoming a couple. And Jim had no time to bond with his baby daughter, which, as we understand from the teaching of Winnicott, is when a couple becomes a family unit. The pressure on families during the war left scars which are still being felt by subsequent generations. Couples, and families, need plenty of energy and a long period to grow together; during the war there was insufficient time for either.

2   Working at a Marriage

Marriage resembles a pair of shears, so joined that they cannot be separated; often moving in opposite directions, yet always punishing anyone who comes between them.

Sydney Smith

What Makes a Family Survive?

To keep up with the mood of the moment popular writers now use the expanding unit, the stepfamily, as the basis for their novels. Joanna Trollope grasps the nettle in this way in her bestselling *Other People's Children* (1998). She paints vivid portraits of the different people caught up in the tangling and untangling of breakups and remarriages. What the adults try to achieve, and what the children actually experience are two very different things. Deborah Moggach's popular BBC drama series *Close Relations* (1998), based on her novel, is a grim picture about an emotionally dysfunctional family. In an interview about the series with Cosmo Landesman in the *Sunday Times* she defends her 'coupling couples' as a tragic portrait of our times. Moggach claims that, 'These days if someone has a relationship that lasts five years, it's considered quite a feat.' These are only two illustrations of the way the media dwells on marriages that *don't* work. There are endless articles and interviews about public figures whose marriages fail. Yet, fortunately, there are many who have had long and successful married lives. Some of these were prepared to share with us the reasons why they thought their marriage had been a success.

Elizabeth Longford, married in 1931, recalled her childhood:

ELIZABETH LONGFORD: *'There were millions of cousins. Nobody talked about divorce. There was no assumption about divorce. People expected their marriage to last. Not everyone was happy, but the marriages lasted.'*

Together Elizabeth and Frank Longford had eight children (and have seen four of those divorce). She quoted Winston Churchill: 'It has been said that democracy is the worst form of government except all other forms that have been tried.' 'The same could be said for marriage', she said. 'Work at marriage? Not Frank and me. But of course, we have changed over the years. He knows my weaknesses, I know them myself, so it's not an insult when he points them out.' Their highly successful marriage demonstrates the unconscious shift which takes place between couples, as they move to keep in step with each other. Both are independent and strong-minded people, and they could hold their own ground without feeling judged or criticised.

DIANA MENUHIN: *'We have been married forty-seven years. There was no time to work at the marriage. Yehudi lived on Cloud Nine. The secret of a long marriage is this: never think of yourself as a lone person, you have to think as a couple, and share.'*

Lady Healey, the well-known biographer, spoke of her marriage to Denis Healey, the former Chancellor of the Exchequer. 'We have now celebrated our Golden Wedding plus one year.' It frightens her, she said, hearing young people talk about marriage and 'how we will divide things up if we get divorced'. She was emphatic: 'My generation expected to stay married.'

EDNA HEALEY: *'Denis and I talked and talked before marriage. We were separated during the war, and decided to wait until it was over to get married. I think you should see your life in stages. I believe mothers should give time to their children when they are young, and when they are grown it's your turn, and you are free.'*

She thinks that today's climate in general doesn't help, 'Jobs are no longer long-term, and neither are marriages.' We asked if she had any advice for a couple starting married life together.

EDNA HEALEY: *'Advice? Yes, bite your tongue over little things – blazing rows are all right. And it is an old saying, but it's wise, "Don't let the sun go down on your wrath."'*

DENIS HEALEY: *'Both partners need to keep strong outside interests too.'*

Terry Waite, the former Beirut hostage, also spoke to us:

TERRY WAITE: *'Frances and I have been married for thirty-three years. I believe there is value in attempting to live to an ideal, to make a lifelong commitment, even if at times it is difficult. This commitment gives security to the children when they need it.'*

Marigold Johnson trained to become a counsellor once her children had left home and at an age when most women think about retiring.

MARIGOLD JOHNSON: *'We married in 1959. Completing the training and working as a counsellor has meant I enjoy and understand so much more what made us behave as we did over the years. It does seem possible to be – as we counsellors say – 'nonjudgmental'. That may be the hardest aspect of sustaining marriage, because things so often seem the other person's fault. But in order to forget (which of course really just means tidying away) you have to forgive and that requires accepting a share of guilt and responsibility. I can't imagine how any divorced couple can forgive each other or ever forget the hurt, let alone the suffering of their children.'*

Johnson – like others we spoke with – felt it was miraculous to spend half a lifetime with one person.

Questions and Answers

When asked in magazines and newspapers and on the Internet, the question 'What makes a family?' brought a plethora of responses; everyone had an opinion.

JEREMY: *'I would certainly like to know more about how some parents and kids stay united.'*

ALAN: *'In order to keep close, heap honest praise on one's spouse and mean it. This show of love and honour can only help project a marriage relationship into an upward spiral which naturally sweeps up the children in its wake.'*

GERALD: *'When I say out loud how smart and clever my wife is, and she is, I am sending my children a very powerful message that she is to be respected and listened to.'*

'Respect' was a word which we heard again and again from those whose marriages had been a success; also emphasis was placed on the need for a consideration for each other. 'Structure', 'lines of demarcation', 'what is proper or improper', and 'consistency in discipline' were terms offered by parents who felt their families to be strong and who wanted to pass on to others their own standards.

We heard repeatedly the view that if there is a warm, loving home, it provides a sound atmosphere that creates positive memories which last a lifetime:

MOLLY: *'I am an old lady now, but I do know this. Families are all about care and must be a place to protect the young and the old, and the sick.'*

NATHAN: *'My marriage went through a very bad patch. I was helped to face the danger ahead when my son aged six asked me, "Are you getting bi-vorced from mum?" I felt it was so sad that a young child should even know what divorce is, even if he didn't know the word. I had promised to love, honour and cherish God's gift to me for better or worse, and I plan to honour that vow by the grace of God. We are now eleven years and counting ...'*

Couples who had stayed married for several years were pleased to have their opinions listened to. Advice came pouring in: 'Be open and affectionate in front of the children.' 'Learn to say sorry, and mean it.' 'Be independent at times, and dependent at others.' 'Take time to decide on marriage and then make it work.' 'It doesn't just happen, make it happen.'

KEN: *'The family that works together, eats together and sings together is a family. Everything else is just people sharing accommodation. A bad image of the 1990s is a houseful of people in separate rooms all watching a different channel on TV.'*

ELIZABETH LONGFORD: *'Marriages are happiest if the wife is engaged. I started my research when my youngest was three years old. But I was always home for their tea. No need for a couple to have everything in common.'*

PETER: *'I tell my wife how pretty she is in the presence of my children, and by doing this, I'm sending a message to my daughters that my wife is the kind of modestly beautiful woman I want them to aspire to be. To my sons also, about the kind of woman I want them to look for in a wife.'*

MARTIN: *'My first marriage broke up when my daughter was only two. I was devastated. Three years on when I fell in love with Marie, I knew I wanted to marry her and build a family together. Still, it set me thinking. Okay the first time round I was young. But what makes a family strong? What had I learnt? I knew I could never survive another breakup.'*

JONATHAN: *'We have been married for twenty-two years. We talk a lot. We chat and chat and chat. And we don't argue. Penny is my great friend as well as being my lover and wife. My first marriage failed because all these good things were completely absent. The constant arguing killed off the whole enterprise. Hence my advice "Don't argue." These are words of experience, more than words of wisdom.'*

Martin, in common with other men and women who talked to us, pondered long and hard about family strengths. His brother, married for ten years, handed on advice saying, 'The road to ruin is paved with good intentions, but good intentions, especially in this family-hostile world we now have, aren't good enough.'

JOSHUA: *'We married in 1950. The possibility that it might not last forever did not enter my mind. Of course we had ups and downs, but that's life.'*

GILBERT, fifty years married: *'Our secret? Just get on with it, and don't bear grudges. If you marry for love, it will see you through.'*

ANDREW, married in 1965: *'Call a spade, a spade. A "fling" or "one night stand" is adultery and a betrayal and should be seen as such.'*

BARRY: *'We married in '69. I think it is incredible to spend a large part of one's life with one person; but I also see that to expect to continue being the same two people who fell in love doesn't leave space to grow separate identities. Different tastes and opinions can all sustain the relationship by making it more rivalrous. It can also make it more equal.'*

Media space is given to broken families and to divorce – mostly in a negative way. It is difficult to find anything about how to try to lessen the pain for the children or the parents. We heard from many men and women desperate to know how to protect or reconstitute a family.

JACK: *'Please help me. My wife has left two husbands and is now leaving me and our children. I don't want my son to learn that it is okay for parents to live apart. It is wrong and I am already seeing the effect on my adolescent stepdaughters by their behaviour and attitude. Our kids are only six and three.'*

Jack was frantic to know how to teach his son the value of human relationships, love and commitment. He felt his stepdaughters were beyond his help and influence.

Becoming a Couple

We frequently heard regrets expressed for not working at a first marriage. 'I didn't think.' 'With hindsight I wasn't mature enough to marry.' 'I expected to be happy ever after, and when we weren't, I left him.'

> PETER: *'Jean and I were so much in love, that working at it was the last thing on our minds. Yet seven years later we both had tears in our eyes when we separated. Where had all that love gone?'*

Many marriages go through difficulties and periods of serious differences. The skill is for a couple to discuss, maybe argue and then negotiate. This is a way towards a mutually agreeable solution. A wise partner can judge the time to withdraw from a previously held position; this can be a strength, not a weakness.

So what does 'work at a relationship' mean? It means noticing the other person's needs, being aware of small changes and not taking anything for granted. After the honeymoon phase many couples reported that they just got on with living. Yet love, there initially, can wither and die if not nurtured. Somehow a kind of lassitude creeps in and changed attitudes are not noticed, subtle warnings are not heeded.

> GRANT: *'Once we had the loving – and then we drifted on with living – and no one was more surprised than I was when Angela walked out on me.'*

Grant told us he asked Angela, 'Why? What did I do?' She told him he had done nothing; that was the point. Somewhere along the way he had stopped talking to her, and listening to her. Angela felt she was as much to blame. She asked herself when did I last really look at Grant? Or try to guess what he was thinking? When did I ask myself, do I make him happy? On reflection Angela concluded it had been only too easy to fall in love with someone else. She had felt excited again, and had delighted in planning small surprises for her lover: 'I felt alive again.'

According to family therapist Warren Colman from the Tavistock Institute of Marital Studies (Colman, 1993) marital therapists frequently ask the question, 'Is there really a marriage here?' 'Is the quality of the relationship sufficient to consider the partners to be *psychologically* married?' Grant and Angela, unhappily, demonstrate the point only too clearly. They had stopped being a couple long before Angela began an affair. The 'we' in their relationship had disappeared, and the 'I' had taken over without them sensing the danger signals which must have been flashing.

> SUE: *'Strange as it may seem an affair saved our marriage. I had a lover but his wife telephoned to say I could keep him. I panicked and had to confess to my husband. We had a lot to talk about, and now looking back it really wasn't important if I compare those few months of illicit passion to our forty years of marriage.'*

Others volunteered their own ideas of a recipe for marriage. In one case the choice of the correct partner had helped to forge a strong relationship.

> MAUREEN: *'I went into therapy for a quite unrelated reason, but during that time I did look at my marriage. It was at the time of our Silver Wedding and I saw very clearly that my choice of Jim as a husband had been very wise. My own father had been very unreliable and had run off when I was two. Jim is a steady headmaster – a "father" to more than two hundred boys and girls. I had spotted something in him when he was just a lad. Reliability is his middle name.'*

Some couples have an unconscious way of detecting change in a partner and moving towards the other's pace and timing. 'We are in tune,' agreed Maureen, 'and after fifty years of being married, it can't have always been the same tune, yet we have kept in step.' Maureen and her husband had been able to forge a strong link which enabled them to move from the newlyweds' romantic young couple, to being young parents, and then to the warm, loving friendship and companionship of their retirement years.

The early years of a marriage appear to be the critical phase, especially when there is a failure to establish a strong foundation upon which the family can be built. This is a period of mutual adaptation if the marriage is to be truly viable. A large number of men and women felt very early in their married life that the marriage just wasn't right and they went on to build a family. If the foundation cracks, the family as a whole suffers. As we heard from Bill, when he felt his marriage stagnate, he left. He felt no compunction to tackle the problems from within the marriage – he was off. But what of Bill's future outlook? He was, perhaps surprisingly, optimistic in the belief that second time around would be different. What of his ex-wife Anne?

ANNE: *'I still cannot believe Bill has gone – especially now. Jenny is just nine months old. I can't see myself ever trusting anyone again, let alone enough to agree to share the rest of my life with them. I see the future as bleak – a single parent with some serial monogamy – but never, ever, believing in one person again and that "it's for life".'*

Perhaps unknowingly Anne puts her finger on the spot: 'for life'. Quite likely the very thought of this, although comforting to some people, causes the Bills of this world to be anxious about making a lifetime mistake, or to feeling trapped. Life expectancy in Britain today is more than seventy-four years for men and nearly eighty for women, whereas in 1901 it was only forty-nine years for men and fifty-two for women, therefore the decision to stay with one partner has an even greater significance.

It is to be hoped we are not seeing the beginning of a new social pattern whereby an adult marrying two or maybe three times will not seem to be so odd or outrageous:

LARRY: *'I married at nineteen for love, at twenty-seven for convenience and at sixty for keeps.'*

But for others it is different, an attitude summed up by Lady Longford. Reflecting in her ninety-second year on her marriage, she comments with a smile, 'The time has flashed past.'

Finding Time to Talk

Successful relationships require quality time. As many parents said, 'Turn off the television one night a week and play and talk instead' or 'share the chores'. Quality time can be created from anything; use all family time as positive time instead of complaining about having to do the jobs in the first place.

JANE: *'I'll bring work home to do after the kids go to bed if I have to, but we are all together at the dinner table.'*

LEO: *'All successful human groups are held together by work and meals.'*

ROSA: *'All the important things I remember from my childhood happened in the kitchen with the centre being the meals.'*

Elizabeth Longford was in no doubt about the importance of early family life for later good communication as an adult.

ELIZABETH LONGFORD: *'Meals together are important – it's where you learn to talk and discuss. A good preparation for marriage.'*

RENE: *'Bring back Sunday lunches for all the family.'*

This may have been a fairly lighthearted comment from Rene, but we see it as an indication of family attitudes and an approach to keeping the family together. Talking and listening must always be a priority. The message that shines through all these comments is the need for a 'family' attitude and what is put high on the personal agenda. If for a family, spending time together in this very busy world is seen as a plus, and something to be valued, there is less likelihood of throwing it away with a casual 'fling' or affair.

BRIAN: *'I saw too many of our friends splitting up. Often it seemed to me for no good reason. I decided to keep a very protective eye on my family and not to make assumptions or to take anything for granted.'*

Families need time spent on them. 'Quality time' is not enough; quantity counts too. It may be difficult to organize, especially for a lone parent or dual-earning couple, but it is only too easy to miss the moment when the communication from a child to a parent is needed and will not wait. The recently-married leader of the Conservative Party has revealed his plans for a successful marriage: he will schedule time with his wife and will spend one weekend a month and every Sunday with her. This is all very well, but one can only hope that it will be more flexible, especially if there are children of the marriage.

CAROLINE: *'One thing I have learnt over the past few years: having children is not compatible with two full-time careers. One full-time and one part-time career is max. So where does that leave me?'*

Bill said the same thing:

BILL: *'Ideally there should be one parent working full-time, possibly with the other working part-time if it is financially worth it. But no family can survive successfully if both parents work full-time. And I'm not just talking about when the kids are little either.'*

Up to the 1950s there was a familiar slogan: 'The family that prays together, stays together.' Families in the 1990s may not put it quite like that. However, the comments we received *did* point to the importance of members of families sharing time and leisure, or interests or common ground or pastimes, with each other. If this happens there is less chance of one member falling through the safety net of the family.

> DAVID: *'I had begun to feel the only value I was to my family was to bring home my pay cheque. We never really spoke or listened to each other. Meeting Mary was like a breath of Spring. I'll never let that happen again. With Mary and the kids we have, and I make certain we have, time to listen to each other's worries as well as the good times. I make sure I never say "not now" or "Dad's too busy to play" like I did with my first family.'*

Lillian spoke to us about the beliefs she and her husband had about bringing up children and the plans they made. Sadly her husband died, and when she met and married Herb (who already had four children) she was startled to find a family without structure or beliefs. Lillian said she had always hoped and intended to bring up a family with a firm composition. But her stepchildren, already very distressed by the divorce and loss of a mother, were in no mood for peaceful contemplation. Lillian said she put in a lot of prayer. She began to build a new extended family which included her own parents and Herb's (at first unwilling) parents to give the children a sense of security, of belonging and of family responsibilities.

> LILLIAN: *'I got the children to see how special each one is, even with all our warts. It shows true love and acceptance, caring and helping, compassion and all that stuff.'*

It was tough going, but Lillian began showing her stepchildren that even if they made mistakes, she and their dad would always love them. She saw the children through years of rebellion, confronted them when they were out of order, let them suffer the consequences, but always let them know they were loved. Lillian's stepchildren are now adults, with children of their own. Lillian says the proof of the pudding is in the eating and she counts herself fortunate to have had the opportunity to bring peace and love to a turbulent family.

Kevin, too, felt when he became a stepfather he became totally involved with a new wife he loved dearly. But she was still suffering (as were her children) from being in a family torn apart by a very stormy divorce on top of years of violence and abuse.

KEVIN: *'I felt I had to start from square one.'*

Kevin and Joyce had a shared task to rebuild their family. The children had been witnesses to their father's lack of control and violence. There had been no respect or liking and the children had responded by becoming totally disruptive and disorderly.

KEVIN: *'It was an uphill job to bring order into the chaos of this family. But Joyce and I worked at it and I began to hold the family together. It was a stormy time, I can tell you. But well worth it when you see the love expressed within our family now.'*

To bring love and respect with you into a 'new family' situation after it has been lost within the original family makes for thoughtful consideration, patience and a strong will to succeed.

PAULA: *'It must start with the relationship with your ex and your husband's. My husband's ex-wife is not perfect, but not as bad as some ex-wives I hear about. I make sure when we do have to have contact, that I'm always polite. I do try to look for the good in her as well as the bad. This helps to create peace in our home on all fronts.'*

The desire to bring about a happy coexistence is in the forefront for many. It is not an easy position to maintain and Jane was desperate when she contacted us.

JANE: *'I am trying to create a stable family unit, but how on earth do I create peace in the valley? We get abusive calls from the kids' mother – she doesn't want them, yet can't leave them alone. I insist that Jim and I (and the kids) are always civil to her. I never rubbish her or speak ill of her – yet her calls are an unwelcome intrusion and very disruptive.'*

These contributions are from men and women determined to keep their families safe and intact from the spreading number of split families. All are actively working to maintain family beliefs to prevent the pain of separation and divorce – especially when one family rift had already been witnessed.

Fallout from Divorce

Nevertheless, the goal that so many loving newlyweds hope they will reach, escapes more couples each year. At times, flight from a truly abusive marriage may be a relief. On the other hand one partner may want to bring this about much to the distress of the other. The breakup is of course more traumatic for all if there are children from the partnership. As each individual parent struggles to come to terms with his or her own feelings about the separation, the children have to cope with tremendous and often heartfelt difficulties. In our previous book, *Where's Daddy?* (Curtis and Ellis, 1996), we showed that the harmful effect on the children of a broken marriage is profound and lasting, whatever the age. Children can be helped, but never spared. Single parenting is hard whether you are the mother or the father, especially as most parents try to compensate for the non-custodial parent. John summed it all up:

> JOHN: *'Single parenthood is very tough. It's hard on both the kids and adults.'*

In a situation where death of a parent is the reason for a family breakdown there is time set aside for both adults and children to grieve. A mourning period is expected and there are rules and customs to be observed. Help and support are freely given by family and friends. A death is final and so acceptance is eventually easier to bear. Then hopefully the recovery can begin.

The death of a marriage is not so clearly defined. Trial separations can be lengthy, and the hope a marriage may be mended can mean keeping the truth secret for some time. For instance, the children can be told, 'Daddy is working abroad for a while.' A parent may ricochet backwards and forwards several times before finally leaving for ever.

For some parents, the thought that the children are deeply affected by the adults' behaviour when they separate is almost too much to bear. And so denial of this problem is one unhappy way of managing the situation.

> NIGEL: *'Jenny was only two when I went, she wouldn't have noticed.'*

> MARK: *'I waited until they were at university before I left.'*

> SARAH: *'I saw them every holiday.'*

These are all ways of trying to sweep aside the grief of the children. Of course, children respond in different ways, and fear, bewilderment, guilt and aggression are but a few of the more obvious signals. In addition, children frequently show signs of yearning for the departed parent and anger towards the resident parent. This is particularly difficult to cope with while keeping the family afloat.

'The Exeter Family Survey' (Cockett and Trip, 1994) into family breakdown found there was 'no disagreement that the children involved are disadvantaged'. Amongst other things, parents are urged to keep the children fully informed, and if possible to talk to the children together. The burden must be on the parents to keep disagreements away from the children, and not to expect the children to act as 'peace or war-maker' with the other parent.

This is to assume that rational, calm discussions take place. The reality is often somewhat different and in the heat of the moment 'talking to the children together' can get lost and they will not be protected.

The pain of separation can be heavier for one parent than the other:

JUDY: 'I had no idea my husband was leaving us. Once he told me he was leaving, he talked non-stop about "falling in love again". He wasn't the one who was grieving about our shattered life – only me and of course the kids did too.'

Judy continued by describing her fear of loneliness and feelings of rejection, magnified, she felt, by her ex-husband's surge of energy and happiness. Her husband had told her he was gay and had found a new partner.

BETTY: 'Our family is a mess. Phil left me for someone else, then he came back a week later saying she had told him to go home as she wouldn't be responsible for two little kids losing their dad. Now I'm depressed and tearful over the marriage, and Phil is in despair and sees his life in ruins. The kids are bewildered by it all. Of course they know something is up.'

JOHN: 'It would have been much easier on us all if June had died instead of running off and leaving us. I could have remembered the good times and told the children lovingly about how our family used to be. Now, all I feel is bitterness and anger. When I talk of their mother this obviously shows, I'm afraid.'

SUZANNE: 'I was ten when my mother left us for Bruce. I went to a convent school where it was very unacceptable to have divorced *parents and my mother was painted as a very scarlet woman. I was desperate and felt so very alone. I took refuge in religion, which is still very important to me. I realize that at forty years old, many of the problems which I suffer from today, both physical and emotional, are caused by the handling of the situation way back then.'*

Changes in Circumstances

Moving house, possibly more than once, and perhaps leaving school and friends behind can be part of the loss experienced by many children when a family breaks up. Britain's explosion of divorces also means two households are needed where one would have done in the past. The increased demand for more housing could not have been predicted twenty-five years ago, when there were only 30,000 divorces a year.

> JEREMY: *'The worst thing that happened when we split up was seeing the children uprooted from their home and school. I left Janet, but I hadn't reckoned on her leaving Hull and moving south to be with her family. I thought it was too many changes at once for the kids.'*

Indeed, it is often the accumulation of losses which has such a detrimental effect on children. Professor Ian Goodyer published a paper in 1994 (*Journal of the Royal Society of Medicine*) on the impact of recent life events in anxious and depressed school-age children. His findings suggest that 'multiple exit events', as he calls major separations, may not exert their effects until late in the child's life. Two or more losses are significantly more likely to be reported in the history of anxious or depressed children.

Jeremy had hoped to work out a shared care arrangement for the children, but this was not to be. He told us he regretted not discussing the details of the breakup more carefully. He realized, too late, that he had assumed Janet would agree to the parenting being shared equally. He was totally shocked when she moved 250 miles away and he could see the children only during the holidays.

The Association for Shared Parenting can be contacted for advice, and on a national and local level they try to influence professionals working with families and decision makers. They will support parents in the task of fulfilling a child's right to the nurture of both parents after a separation or divorce.

Finance

Most young couples with children are on a tight budget, and with the additional cost of two households and expenses we can understand the increased pressure on parents after a separation. The wrangling over finances can continue for years.

> HENRIETTA: *'We drifted apart. It was inevitable I suppose, because we didn't care enough right from the beginning. We were having trouble financially too. Ken couldn't keep up the mortgage payments for the house we lived in. When he left, I moved with the children to a flat where we felt cosy and safe. It was difficult, though, moving the children to the local school. What I couldn't forgive him for was when I found out he was buying a good-sized home to put his new wife and baby into just months later.'*

> JACK: *'I felt torn into bits. I wanted to keep up my financial deal with my first family, but my new wife and children began to be a drain on me too. Wherever I put my money it seemed to be the wrong place for someone. Money can only be stretched so far. I moved from feeling guilty towards my first wife and children to seeing them as bloodsuckers, and I know my second wife does as well.'*

Jack's sentiments about his despair over money were echoed repeatedly; problems over finance surfaced frequently as an issue. Financial arrangements often became the concrete reason for continued acrimony and at times there seemed to be an unconscious element in forcing the ex-partner to pay. The reality was of course there; loss of financial security and of a standard of living are two of the most unpleasant after-effects of a divorce. Where there is a new second family to support the strain is increased further.

> MARIA: *'The pain goes on way past the actual divorce. When my husband left me and my two children for another woman I felt so shocked and hurt I wondered if I'd ever get over it. For the most part I think I'm doing well, keeping together a home, the children's school and home life, part-time work and a fairly busy social life for myself. Despite my ex's on-and-off interest in our children, his new wife and their three children, I have managed to keep the contact going with my two and their dad. But then there is the straw that breaks the camel's back. This time it is lack of money again and I*

feel desperate. I ask myself why is it so painful so long after the break? Why can't I let go of an unhappy marriage? Will I ever get over the past and be able to start again? Or is it my ex who can't let go? Why is it so important to him to still have financial control over me?'

When Clare was left with no income and two children of two and three years old, she had to turn to the state for support.

CLARE: *'Money was very tight indeed but the children have come through the dreadful situation of divorce in great form because they felt so very loved, secure and knew that I was always there for them. It was so hard for the children to live in the same town as their dad, his new partner and their children who went on holidays. He got away with it because his new wife's family paid for all their treats.'*

Clare says she feels proud of the way she and the children have learnt to value other important things in life. They grow their own vegetables, and Clare says they have become truly aware of nature. 'We can't afford holidays, but it doesn't cost anything to sleep out in our yard in the summer and talk about the stars.' Clare's face glowed when she described the pleasures she and her children have in walking beside the river, visiting the library, and singing songs together.

CLARE: *'The lesson my kids are learning is that money cannot buy everything, and that we can find happiness in each other.'*

JENNY: *'I am frantic about what changes in benefit will mean. I can't believe there is all this business about looking after other people's children being a proper job, but looking after your own isn't, and you ought to get a proper job.'*

Emotional Struggles

It is not only money that cannot be stretched. Fathers reported that however hard they tried and however good the intentions were, it was difficult to maintain the psychological and emotional connection with their first family – especially when their subsequent partner and children needed their time and affection as well.

Janet Walker (Professor at the Centre for Family Studies, University of Newcastle-upon-Tyne) carried out a recent research study in

1997 for the Joseph Rowntree Foundation devoted to fathers six years after their divorce. The findings showed that

> Fathers had to renegotiate their role as a father following the break-down of the marital relationship in order to successfully continue to have contact with their children. As nationally most children of divorce reside with their mothers and some 40% of their fathers lose contact within a few years of the divorce, this is a significant issue.

During Walker's research it emerged that the major difficulty facing a father was in this renegotiating of his role. It comes as no surprise that the fathers most successful in achieving good contact were often those who had not established new partner relationships. The most shocking outcome of this research is uncovering the belief that many fathers did not realize until some time after the divorce that they needed to talk to their children about relationships and roles.

Families Need Fathers (FNF) is the principal organization providing help for fathers who no longer live with their children. An active charity established more than twenty years ago, it promotes the view that after a divorce the father gets a very raw deal, and that children suffer because of this. This organization is a very powerful voice trying to help fathers to maintain contact, sometimes against all odds. According to FNF, fathers are now beginning to overcome problems much more successfully than previously believed as the value of a father in a child's life is more appreciated. Meanwhile, they work to increase public awareness of the problems facing children and parents who experience family breakdown.

> KELVIN: 'I tried, I really tried, to keep involved with Terry and Joey, but once my two kids from my second marriage began to need more of me I felt overwhelmed. Something had to go and it was time and interest in Terry and Joey's life. It didn't help that my second wife insisted I spent time with our children and I had less to give – in every sense of the word – to my older children.'

This is a point which will emerge more clearly in other chapters: if a new partner feels threatened or is jealous of the time and money spent on children of a previous relationship it is only too easy to take advantage of a position of power. This is often seen and felt in a new relationship and used to discourage the visiting parent from maintaining good close contact with his or her children. However, we also heard from fathers who continued to visit their children, despite remarriage and new families.

FRANK: *'I often felt totally worn out going between two families. Nobody seems to realize that to leave one family each Saturday, drive a hundred miles to pick up your other kids, hang out with them for the day, have a fight with your ex at handover time and then drive back a hundred miles to go home and to be asked to put your other kids to bed is too much. My new wife always wants me to prove to her and my two little boys that I hadn't become so involved with my kids from my first marriage that I had nothing left over for them.'*

GEORGE: *'I did not divorce my kids and after Jessica and I split up I insisted I saw the children frequently, and was part of their lives. I wasn't to know just how difficult this was to do. On paper it looked simple – in reality it was impossible. I don't understand how I did not foresee how painful and difficult it would all become.'*

Families who are fragmented or who are in a process of transition can feel bewildered and lost. The most common trap to fall into is to hope that because there are so many broken families, one more will somehow not be so painful. Anyone working alongside families needs to be on the lookout for signals which show that a family is struggling. This is especially so where the constitution of a particular family is unconventional in a way still not generally accepted by society.

When the first marriage has formally ended, what of the future? How can the new family regroup in a successful way to minimize the stress, especially for the children?

3   The Family after Divorce

Growing up is not all honey for the child, and for the mother it's often bitter aloes.

D.W. Winnicott

The New Family

CHRISSY (divorced with a ten-year-old daughter): *'The new family? What new family? The family doesn't exist anymore, does it?'*

Yet from another mother, more positive words:

RACHEL: *'A family is where there is love and togetherness, and we do have that.'*

Whereas we used to know what makes a family, the guidelines are now blurred and there no longer may be a set pattern. The world at large, including politicians, lawyers, professional people in all walks of life and the media cast a new slant upon an institution which was once thought to be unchangeable. Surprisingly, the bishops of the Church of England no longer believe cohabiting couples are necessarily committing a sin. They are convinced the *quality* of the relationship is more important than its legal and religious status. The Bishop of Hereford is quoted as saying, 'Christian people should recognize the realities of social change.' Yet within the Church there is confusion. The Archbishop of Canterbury urges the government to support the family. An open letter to Mr Blair, signed also by Cardinal Hume and Chief Rabbi Dr Jonathan Sacks, is proof of the anxiety of these three religious leaders about the state of the family.

The Irish bishops recognize the reality of one-parent families when they say, 'The Christian understanding of the family is of mother, father and children united in a bond of married love ... This ideal is not always the visible reality. Many families suffer the pain of absence or brokenness. These are true families also, whose love is often deepened with suffering as they struggle towards wholeness' (1994, *Cherishing the Family*, Dublin: Veritas).

At a recent conference, the Conservative Party with one voice called for tolerance of cohabitation, while their leader, William Hague, was reaffirming the Tories as 'guardians of family values'. And New Labour has put the spotlight on single mothers with its Welfare to Work policy, of which the principal effect is to undermine the confidence of stay-at-home lone parents. The message seems to be that there is no value to be had from a mother looking after her young children at home, even if that is what she wants to do. This new policy dismisses the value of the full-time mother, especially in single-parent households. What About the Children? (WATCH?), a national charity formed in 1993, aims to raise public awareness of the importance of the time a mother cares for her young children at home. They believe that policy makers ignore the risk of psychological damage caused by mothers returning to work before their babies are emotionally ready for the separation. The improved childcare promised by Blair's government – a government which maintains that it is the 'champion of the family' – seems to imply that anyone can replace a parent; that all that is necessary is for children to be minded. But bringing up a child is more than just about 'childcare' – being minded – as any parent will vouch for.

> MAE: *'It is not as simple as the politicians would like it to be. In my Gingerbread group six out of eight of us are on a course. One woman has had to wait sixteen years to begin one. She had no child support earlier, and had to wait until her children grew up. They would all like to be earning, but they all know their duty is to be there for their kids when they are young. But we are all looking to the future.'*

The Child Poverty Action Group is concerned that all lone mothers are seen as one group, without any allowance for different circumstances. Therefore such statistics as, 'Three out of ten lone parents cannot work because of their own ill health or disability', and 'A quarter of lone parents have a child with long-term illness or a disability' are not taken into account.

We used to be shocked by the behaviour of Hollywood film stars and pop idols; now their behaviour is universal and we are fed a daily diet of the way royals and cabinet ministers engage in the painful, insensitive dance of replacing partners. Those holding the most tolerant attitudes were astounded when the Foreign Secretary moved his mistress into his official residence and announced his decision to take her abroad on official government business. Questions were asked in the House of Commons about 'cost to the taxpayer', but the cost to the minister's wife, children and mother received no official comment. It was left to his eighty-five-year-old mother-in-law to observe, 'I thought they had been happy. It is terrible after twenty-eight years.'

Is it really a case of out with the old, in with the new? For the one who decides to make a second family, very possibly with the support of a fresh relationship, there will be the energy and impetus to do just that. But it will not be so easy for the other partner if he or she was content with the 'old' way of life, and ill-prepared for the 'new'. When one parent leaves the family for any reason, the remaining parent and children have to find ways of coping with the loss and the changes in their lives.

> AUDREY: *'For me it was the sudden shock of Alan leaving after fifteen years of married life. Then it was the misery of watching our three children truly suffer from the effect of seeing their lives change so abruptly.'*

Parents who have had to deal with a family breakdown often expressed the opinion that not nearly enough is written or spoken about the pain of the children. 'My nine-year-old became withdrawn and lost her zest for life at school.' 'Timmy wouldn't talk about the situation, but at the same time the school reported his aggressive behaviour and his poor attitude to work.' 'Lily has ME – or is it grief she is suffering from?'

Following the breakup, there may be relief at first, particularly if the period leading up to the split has been stormy or violent. But, there are more problems ahead for the mother who is opposed to the father having contact because she fears for her own safety and that of the children. She is embarking on a legal road paved with difficulties.

And as the 'new' family endeavours to settle back into everyday life the trauma and shock make themselves felt. Whatever the marriage had been like there is always grief that something which had been entered into with enthusiasm and love did not grow but died. After all, each broken relationship is a failed love-story.

> ANNA: *'I am on my own now with a teenage son. I don't believe I could ever love again, although I know it would be good for my boy to see me loved.'*

So how do you find a way of creating a family from the pieces left behind? We heard from both men and women who had stopped to take a long hard look at their situation, and to see what they could make of their life in the future.

> LAURA: *'It's not easy to create a new family when you have to live in the shadow of the old because of finance. But I tell myself, "home is where the heart is", and the children and I hold fast to that.'*

Single-handed

According to Single Parent Action Network (SPAN) 23 per cent of all families with children are lone-parent families – which makes a total of 1.3 million single parents in Britain. How many of these men and women have had 'single parent' status thrust upon them? Some women do choose to be single mothers and to create a family on their own, but this is by no means the majority, and those that do make this choice still find themselves faced by single-parent issues. The Information Officer for SPAN spoke with us:

> ANNIE: *'Despite the fact that single parents are struggling against isolation and with finance, being a single-parent family is becoming the norm. Families are changing and SPAN is working hard to chip away at the prejudice and to create a more equal society.'*

This organization not only helps the single parents themselves, but also any relatives who need advice concerned with a family, and they provide information and details about local support groups.

> PAULINE: *'I am a single mother by choice. I have one child through adoption, but it is tough, even if I don't have all the usual problems, like an ex or dealing with a death. I have never regretted my choice. I would do it again in a heartbeat. I love my life.'*

> MAE: *'I left my husband after twenty-three years of marriage. Of course it wasn't all my husband's fault, but I had to go and took my youngest daughter with me. I had lost my identity, and eventually after a lot of thought I found the strength to leave. It is hard, and I couldn't foresee all the problems I would have.'*

> ANNA: *'I am a thirty-two-year-old widow and I am appalled at the prejudice I meet and the things people say about a single mother on her own. The hardest part is doing everything alone, and the eternal struggle over money. On the plus side there are no differences of opinion over disciplining.'*

> ALISON: *'I was desperate. I had a two- and a three-year-old, very little money and felt the pressure to get to work. One look at nurseries told me that my job was to stay at home and care for my kids who were already bewildered by losing a father and their home.'*

JENNY: *'It would be nice to have a partner and to share – but it's not the end of the world. I am okay with my two kids. It is certainly not a man and a woman and children that make a family.'*

The responsibility of being a single parent, with daily decisions about bringing up a child and often trying to balance a tight budget, is a daunting one.

MAE: *'Money was a huge problem. We had a private arrangement, and I worked part time. Then the Child Support Agency got involved and that made things worse, much worse. My husband wasn't speaking to me, and my daughter had to deal with the bad atmosphere between us. I became ill with the strain. Yes, the CSA made things much worse.'*

The Single Parent Action Network was established in 1990 as part of the European Poverty Programme. It is a multiracial organization run by single parents working to improve the lives of one-parent families in the UK and Europe. They strive to band together to make changes in discriminating policies and to change attitudes in order to prevent one-parent families struggling against poverty and isolation. SPAN has been most vocal in voicing its dismay at the thought of government policy trying to push 800,000 single parents into the labour market, where jobs do not exist. Of course, there are single parents who would like to get to work, but the dilemma of how to balance this while underpinning a secure family life is a bleak one. The policy makers do not seem to take on board that many children of one-parent families are already suffering from a family breakup and need the constant love and care of the resident parent.

RACHEL: *'It's all very well talking about the difficulties for children of divorce, but that's what it's like, and that's a fact. I didn't want it to be that way. I am still grieving over all my lost plans and broken dreams, and I have to be a parent to three young children. I feel totally betrayed. I was just chucked for a younger woman. I feel the pain of that, day in and day out.'*

All the evidence gathered over the years about the importance of caring for a child – especially children under the age of three – is too often disregarded when there is pressure on a mother to work outside the home. Since the young child's experience of early mothering has a lifelong impact on his ability to make future close relationships, society needs to be aware of the consequences for the next generation if this is not valued. Children should have consistency of care, individual attention and prompt response to distress. Especially after a divorce – which at best means partial loss of a parent – the importance of the presence of the resident parent cannot be emphasized too strongly.

What About the Children? submitted a resolution for debate at the National Council of Women's Conference calling upon the government to ensure that mothers of children under three should have the financial support to equip them to meet their children's emotional needs during those early years. Perhaps surprisingly, the resolution was not carried. However, a very large number of the delegates abstained from voting. Doreen Goodman, the President of WATCH? says that in time the young mothers of today will wake up to the fact that we have *known* for a long time about the importance of mothers caring for their young children, but we have not reinforced and supported this belief. Mrs Goodman believes it is equivalent to society ignoring for years the danger that smoking causes disease. It is often when at her (or his) lowest ebb, a lone parent has to care for the children. If, at this time there is no support given, there may be little energy to look after the children properly, and the long-term effect is catastrophic.

Part of the work of WATCH? is to bring attention to 'Attachment Disorder' (recognized by the World Health Organization in the International Classification of Diseases). When a baby cries the mother responds with affection and confidence. If the relationship between mother and baby is a happy one, the baby can then reach out to other members of the family and so to the outside world. Therefore, again we see the importance of supporting the early mother/baby relationship, hopefully leaving her free of financial worries and other anxieties. For some – perhaps a very reluctant partner of a divorce – it is not the legal, but the psychic divorce which is often the hardest to manage, and takes the longest to come to terms with, and may mean a mother on her own is distracted from caring for her baby. If the baby does not have this basic happy experience, the seed is sown for the development of 'Attachment Disorder' (AD) which can wreak havoc within the family and the community.

WATCH? encourages policies to prevent AD since this condition is difficult to reverse in a child whose early attachment relationship failed to meet his or her needs. If a child does not have the experience of that healthy loving care within him- or herself, the ability to form a good relationship in later life is almost impossible. Sheila Switzer, when she was vice-chairman of WATCH? prepared a paper on behalf of the organization to comment on *Child Health in the Community: A*

Guide to Good Practice, a consultation draft put out by the Department of Health in March 1995. Several points she raised then, for example, that health education in schools should deal with the importance of family life and the vital roles of both mother and father, are now beginning to be recognized policy. The paper underlined the value of help, advice, and support to vulnerable young mothers and referred again to the monumental work more than forty years ago by John Bowlby for the World Health Organization, and his research showing the adverse effects of maternal deprivation. Sheila Switzer also drew the government's attention to the fact that taking note of all the evidence, a mother contemplating an early return to work after childbirth should be warned of the danger of lifelong damage to her infant. This may be especially so if the infant encounters a large number of different carers in the course of the week, since this could damage the child's capacity to form human bonds throughout life. The paper states categorically that, 'this information should also be included in the training advice and counselling for child minders and those whose children attend day-care, and that this training should be mandatory'.

Peter Wilson, Director of Young Minds, the mental health charity for children, spoke to us about the changes in family life brought about by the fact that previous existing structures are not in place. He believes that as there are more pressures on families, and on broken families, there is a link with the increasing number of children being diagnosed with 'Attention Deficit Hyperactivity Disorder'.

PETER WILSON: *'Children who are restless or fidget and with poor communication are displaying symptoms of the absence of reliability of care. There is more cut and thrust to life today, and dual earning families add pressure onto the children, lone parents struggle in poverty, and these facts have an effect on child rearing. If a parent is more "on the edge", kids worry, and parental care is more fraught. Children need a sense of containment, security and reliability and continuity around them. Pressure from the outside world and on the parents means there is less time for them to give devoted care to their children.'*

Wilson, a child psychotherapist, endorsed the fact that divorce does affect children very profoundly; especially, he believes, if they are between the ages of seven and eleven when their need for order and structure is paramount. In addition, their loyalty to both parents is stretched beyond endurance. It is not only the professionals and experts who understand this:

HELEN: *'I saw how my son Ian, who is eight, really suffered when we split. At times I thought he would break in half. I know his heart is broken.'*

MAE: *'I know all the research says it is best for a child to be with its mother from birth to three. That's a fact. All the lone parents I know would love to go back to work in time. I think it's dreadful all this publicity about the drive to get young mothers to work. They do.'*

PAM: *'I know there are lots of other one-parent families, it's just that I hadn't realized how hard it is to do everything on your own. Tom didn't play the father role really, but he was here to mind the kids when I popped to the shops. It's hard to be a mum and a dad.'*

The First Months

Karen told us how difficult she had found it to maintain family life when her partner left her with a five-year-old son. Not only did she have to mourn the death of her marriage and the life she had planned on, but had to look to the welfare of Jack who was grieving for the loss of his father.

KAREN: *'I felt so alone. It's so hard to be just one parent and make all the decisions. I know I clung to my little boy. A couple of years later when he was seven, I realized I could not, and should not, bring him into my bed at night just because I was lonely. What I did, was to make a tremendous effort to meet other "only" parents and invite them to share meals and outings. I found that this way my son and I felt more of a family. I could also discuss with others in a similar position decisions I had to make.'*

GEORGE: *'My wife left me with a two-year-old son, and in answer to your questions, we're doing just fine.'*

We could see he was doing well physically and we asked him how he was coping emotionally.

GEORGE: *'I'm holding together quite well as it happens. Anger is a damn good glue.'*

When hearing George's comment, Kelly, a single mother on her own, wanted to add: 'Love is also a damn good glue, I know, it keeps us together.' George went on to tell us that his parents provided 'good strong extra family support'. Although George was the main carer he made sure his son received loving attention from grandparents and aunts, which contributed hugely to a sense of stability and belonging. George found that support from other fathers through the organization Families Need Fathers was invaluable. Not only did George link up with other fathers, but they could share outings with other dads and kids.

GEORGE: *'It all helps Jack feel part of a larger family.'*

We're a Family

After the loss of the familiar family unit it may take some time to feel established as a new family:

EMMA: *'At thirty-nine and after seven years of marriage I found myself a single parent. I didn't choose to be one and, would you believe, at first could only think I must find a new partner. It took two years and many tears for me to realize that mum, dad and kids are not the only combination to make up a "family".'*

CATHERINE: *'On the way back from school with my daughter and her friend, both four years old, I heard my daughter explain that her daddy didn't live at home with her but with another mummy and little girl. Her friend responded with "Oh does he love someone else then?" I nearly ran into the car in front, I was so shocked to hear the words that I hadn't let myself even think, spoken by a four-year-old.'*

Catherine went on to tell us that the shock she felt helped her to concentrate on the reality of the situation: that she was alone with her daughter – and together they were now the family.

Wendy, who found sole responsibility draining, decided upon a different approach to recreate a family.

WENDY: *'I hated being a "lone" parent. I searched until I found a man in a similar position and quite frankly we made a deal. I cared for his home and child and he in turn cared for me and my child. It worked well for a couple of years.'*

We were told of the prejudice single parents can feel directed towards them, particularly when they are struggling to keep afloat.

MAE: *'People don't realize there are lots of reasons for becoming a lone parent. So all this anti-one-parent families is just prejudice. My mother is one, because she is a widow. I am one because I chose to separate and my second daughter is a single parent. She works part time and is studying. And she has to pay her own fees. So we are all different but most people don't choose to see things that way. Our ages range from eighty to twenty-four.'*

KATIE: *'I was hurt by one family who, with four children, saw themselves as "the ideal family". And they betrayed their belief that my daughter and I are not! They hinted that any occasion for Alice to go and stay with them in "a proper family" would be beneficial to her.'*

BARBARA: *'I dated a man twice, and then he rang me to tell me he didn't want to be a father to my children. I hadn't asked him to be! I am a working professional woman and I can support myself and my children. People make false assumptions about a single mum – they all think you are on the look-out for another man. I wasn't – I knew we were a family on our own.'*

MILLIE: *'I was so ashamed when my ex-husband left me and my daughter. I felt everyone would think there was something wrong with us. My self-confidence plummeted. I had very little money, I was depressed and tearful and looked awful. I hardly had any contact with anyone. Eventually anger became a spur and I decided I wouldn't let him get away with destroying us. My duty was to provide a family life for my daughter and I'm proud to say I think I have done it. Life is certainly different but we are a family and in many ways happier now than when I lived with a bullying husband. A family is where you feel safe.'*

ROSIE: *'Gingerbread was my saviour. My husband left me after twenty years of marriage with a son of fifteen. My husband was the driver in our family, so when he went the car did too. I thought "Right, I will learn to drive", and I did at forty-five years old. The next time we met after I had passed was truly "in your face". The hardest thing was the first of everything – first Christmas on our own, first birthday – but my son and I are much closer now. We go on outings with Gingerbread, and I go on courses they run. I have a life! Of course we are a family.'*

ANNA: *'I am a single mum. I felt a family from the moment Josh was born.'*

ANGELA: *'Out of the blue my husband walked out and I was on my own with three young children. I wanted to stay in bed and put the covers over my head. After one sleepless night I suddenly thought, "What am I doing?" He didn't make us a family, the closeness and love between the kids and me do that. We are still a family, and a loving one.'*

HELEN: *'When I realized I had lost the family I thought was so concrete, I took the kids and moved to Sussex. I'd always wanted to live in the country and felt we could make a fresh start somewhere different. We are indeed a new and different family.'*

Helen found support and quickly established a feeling of belonging to a village community. She reached out, and was given much in return from her new neighbours.

From different sources we heard of a groundswell of opinion to combat the damage done to families by labels. And Angela and Helen's positive thinking goes a long way to combat the image of 'single parent' or 'one-parent family' or 'unsupported mother'. In contrast the media is still prejudiced: reports of an alleged rape of a nine-year-old girl by boys of her peer group in a primary school in London in 1997 without exception drew attention to the number of children at the school who lived in single-parent families.

GLORIA: *'I will not let us be called a single-parent family. My son has two parents – how could it be otherwise? Divorce doesn't change that.'*

LAURIE: *'My ex and I both want what is best for our son. We make sure he knows that he has one home and "visits" daddy's home. We think this gives more stability. We are divorced, but Sammy has two parents who care for him and love him.'*

NAOMI: *'When my partner deserted me I considered my position very carefully. I had four children to provide for, financially and emotionally, and I knew I would be very stretched. What I did was to find another woman in a similar position and we combined forces. We became a very united family. Different, but safe and loving. We are not anti-men, just two mothers still hurting from the treatment by their men.'*

It is not always the mother who is on her own with children to care for:

BRIAN: *'My wife died last year unexpectedly. I have a daughter of eleven years old and she seems to be coping well. But I thought it better for Bella to go off to boarding school in September, and chose a school because it is small, more a large family than a school. Bella's a lucky girl because it will be like she has lots of sisters – better because she can choose them. I can have her home any weekend we like, and as I travel quite a bit for work it's best all round. At the moment my mother-in-law picks Bella up from school but it is getting a bit much for her at seventy-four.'*

Brian went on to comment that he feels ready to make the best of the situation because most widowed men are more likely to be in their sixties, and he is only forty-five and in good health. He is happy to have a very active social life.

BRIAN: *'It's not what we had, or what I would have chosen, but my daughter and I are most certainly a family, with the help also of my mother-in-law.'*

JOE: *'My wife died when Lily was five and Hannah three. Within weeks of her death friends and family were urging me to think of remarrying. No one believed I could look after the girls on my own. "They need a mother" was the message I got over and over again.'*

Joe went on to tell us of the very real difficulties he had, but he was convinced he could be both a mother and a father to his little girls.

JOE: *'After about three years people grudgingly admitted I was coping and we were all okay. That's when the pressure really started. "Joe, those girls need a mother to help them become women" and "Joe, they will need to talk to a woman." It was as if my family and friends couldn't bear to see us as a unit – we were complete. As it happened, it was another five years before I met and fell in love with my second wife. I felt everyone breathed a sigh of relief. They had us boxed up neatly again. We were a family before Molly died, when I was a widower with the girls and after I remarried. But between wives we were not seen like that, but as a troubled dysfunctional family.'*

Support from Family and Friends

Becoming a lone parent requires thinking completely anew a situation for which there has usually been no preparation.

> MARK: *'My wife left me and wanted to take the kids. I fought every inch of the way, but the chief sticking point was how could I work and look after three small children?'*

Mark went on to describe how he called upon family and friends to help out.

> MARK: *'That was okay for a while, but people have their own lives and I realized I was asking too much. That was when I had to give in and let them go and live with their mother and her new man. The children hate it but what could I do?'*

> MAE: *'I belong to Gingerbread – a group for lone parents. We all help each other out.'*

> GRACE: *'Right, I thought, I'll make a family for my son, and I have. It includes my mother, plus an elderly neighbour, and Harry who looks after the garden. Harry's only child is gay, so he has no grandchildren.'*

Grace also described how she goes on family activity holidays where a family like hers is the norm and 'the appearance of two parents plus children would be a total oddity'.

Lynda wanted to speak to us from her, now, adult point of view. She was four years old when her parents divorced. There were very strong family ties in the neighbourhood and her grandparents (her father's parents) lived nearby.

> LYNDA: *'My mother made a great effort to make sure we continued to see our grandparents and that they were a big part of our lives. We would just phone first to make sure my Dad wasn't there. They spent Christmas morning with us, and we would walk to their home after school sometimes.'*

The message from Lynda was loud and clear: even if keeping children in contact with their grandparents is complicated, it is worth the trouble. Lynda was very much aware of the contribution of her own grandparents:

LYNDA: *'They really helped to keep us going as a family after Dad left. It was bad enough losing a dad, but I don't know where we would be if we had lost Gran and Grandad too. They became part of our new family.'*

SALLY: *'They mean so much to our lives. The love of a grandparent is like no other. My child is now sixteen months old and I've talked my parents into moving to the south. I want her to have grandparents around. With them, we felt as complete a family again as we could.'*

Frequently we heard of the value of grandparents after a divorce, and their part in helping to create the new family. (In Chapter 6 we hear more about grandparents and the importance of their relationship with their grandchildren.) In the heat of the moment, anger may mean that by punishing the 'ex' his or her parents get the flack. Actually, denying the children the right to see their other grandparents can only deprive them of an important part of their family network, however unpalatable this may seem. Keeping your children in touch with their 'other' grandparents may be hard work at times, yet it can be invaluable as we hear from Diana:

DIANA: *'We would have been devastated if we had lost Granny and Grandad as well as my father. Looking back I realize it can't have been easy for Mum, but she never made us feel they were not still part of our family. Even without Dad.'*

JOANIE: *'After Len went I wanted to punish all his family. I began to regret it and one day stopped the car by my ex-mother-in-law and you should have seen the joy on her face when she saw the boys. We have never looked back. We never discuss Len, and I feel they are still a mum and dad to me as well as loving, helpful grandparents.'*

If Joanie had continued to 'punish' her in-laws, the children would also have been the losers and Joanie was able to realize this. She values their contribution as she underpins her new, smaller family.

Roger, too, had to call upon those around when Brenda left him and took his daughter to live with Brenda's boyfriend.

ROGER: *'That was shocking enough, but what happened then was even worse. As we wrangled over access, I got a letter from Brenda's solicitor accusing me of child sexual abuse. While it was being sorted – and it took months – I could see my daughter only if accompanied by an approved person. This meant each weekend my mother or sister had to be with me for the day if I was to see Polly. I will never forgive Brenda for what she did. Not for leaving me but for making those cruel accusations. They were nonsense, of course, but I had many fears, that people might have doubts about me. Polly was too young I hope to understand but she was badly affected by the rows which always took place whenever I collected or returned her. God knows where I would have been without the support of my family.'*

Roger continued telling us that despite these difficulties he felt that each weekend he could create a family around himself and his daughter, with the help of his parents and sister. He summed up: 'I lived for the weekends.'

With the continual increase in residential mobility, families with young children often lack the support of an extended family.

EMILY: *'Even though I did not grow up with an extended family, I miss having that for my daughter and myself.'*

In common with many other single parents Emily found a surrogate family: she turned to the Church. Like others she felt 'held' by the community of the Church in a way she had always dreamed of being from a family.

EMILY: *'We have Church lunches once a month, and there the ages run from two to eighty. I miss them like my own family when I don't see them.'*

What Makes a Family?

The composition of families alters over the years, and adjustments need to be accepted. When thinking about what makes a family, many men and women, as we have already heard, have realized that their views have had to shift. Robert can look with pleasure at the changes he has noticed.

ROBERT: *'When Sandra and I married we became a family. We chose to have children and were blessed with six. They are now grown, and as they move away to start their own families by marrying first and then duplicating the process by teaching their children by example, I will be left with my best friend, my wife, my family. I value the "old" family we had and I look forward to my "new" family.'*

Dale said he felt the word 'family' can be broadened to include any conceivable construction.

DALE: *'The family of three is close to what I consider a good one. Physical needs are met, and the emotional needs fulfilled as best we can.'*

Dale told us it differed greatly from the family he grew up in: divorced parents, a parade of 'fathers' and parenting by absence. The experience was difficult but he went on:

DALE: *'As my brothers and sisters grew we became close to each other and more like a family. The difficulties we experienced together made us strong. Every day I make a point of valuing my family to myself. I know just how lucky I am.'*

Dale was not the only one to tell us that he thought children of divorced parents had one advantage over children from an intact family; they had learnt hard lessons of life, and were perhaps better prepared to face the world as they grew up, and to appreciate what they have.

DAPHNE: *'I don't know if this is a new idea or not. I believe you need familiar experiences to share, perhaps around family holidays. It is these events that memories are made of. Mark them, call them rituals if you like, as you drag out the same Christmas decorations year after year. It binds you all together. That way children are less likely to go off and find rituals of their own in a cult – or with druggies.'*

Not just death and divorce, there can be other reasons for a mother to look after the home and family on her own. Diana Menuhin had two stepchildren and two children from her marriage to the celebrated violinist.

DIANA MENUHIN: *'How did I keep the family together when Yehudi was away so much? Well, you just do it. Of course it was difficult, and I became mother and father, grandmother, grandfather, stepmother and step-grandfather to them all. And I tried to be with him as often as I could. I am eighty-five years old now, but feel ninety-five. Perhaps all that "doing" is the reason I feel so tired.'*

More likely it was Lady Menuhin's sense of humour combined with a devotion to duty which saw her through.

DIANA MENUHIN: *'Yes, discipline helped, but it is no good paddling upstream. Go with it, and get on with the job in hand. I had discipline instilled in me as a child from my Edwardian mother, then the discipline of ballet, and from a background of Christian Science.'*

Perhaps the most extreme case of mothers being forced to take all the responsibility on their own is when a husband is away in a war zone or in prison; in these circumstances, with all the troubles involved, the burden can be very heavy.

LILY: *'I often think back to my gran who looked after quite a brood when her husband was off fighting in the war. Women banded together then, and kept the home fires burning. They had a common cause, I suppose.'*

SALLY: *'How to keep a family together when your husband is in prison? With difficulty. I didn't know anyone else in the same boat and believe me the stigma spills over onto the kids. I moved nearer my parents, and that helped a lot.'*

DORRIE: *'When my husband was sent to prison I wanted my kids to know that as bad as things seemed at the time, we were going to get through this together. We all felt the hole he left. We were going to be a family when he came home and the kids needed to know we would remain one while he was gone.'*

To all intents and purposes Adrianna looked like a lone parent from the outside. In fact, as she told us, appearances can be deceptive.

ADRIANNA: *'I had an affair with a Catholic priest and when I fell pregnant, despite using contraceptives, he urged me to have the baby adopted.'*

Adrianna did not do this, and in the event the affair lasted and another daughter was born. Today, she runs Sonflower, a helpline for other women involved in relationships with priests.

Changing Attitudes

These men and women have found alternative ways of creating and appreciating a new family life. They have moved from the more conventional family – father, mother and children living under one roof – into different variations. No longer are one-parent families prepared to fade into the background; they have a right to be accepted by the community. Banding together by joining such organizations as SPAN, Gingerbread and Families Need Fathers helps to provide support and information which are often desperately needed. All these organizations will give advice about finance, debts and sometimes where to go for a holiday.

It appears that the reason why a more unconventional family unit has become a 'new' family does have a bearing upon society's attitude towards it. A woman who has set out to have a child or children without being in a stable relationship, or after being left on her own, will find a fair amount of prejudice towards her situation. A widow, on the other hand, will find that there is more sympathy shown to her plight.

However, although there may be initial sympathy and support for a family when one spouse leaves, it does not really help a person through the loneliness and bereavement which follows a painful separation. Tracy discovered that invitations can soon dry up for a single parent:

TRACY: 'The phone never rang. I was so pleased when I was invited to a lunch with the words "and bring your young man". The look on the face of my hostess when I turned up with twelve-year-old Tom said it all. I had really got it wrong.'

CILLA: 'Friends were good at saying "you must come over" or "I'll ring", even "Come to supper and bring your new man." Not so easy when you haven't been out at all for months.'

The death of a partner is likely to arouse more immediate help, but people have busy lives and a newly bereaved or separated spouse can also be left to cope alone. As we have seen, Joe told us some of the problems he came up against as a lone father after his wife died. He felt no one believed he could keep a family going on his own, and without exception friends and relations urged him to remarry as soon as possible. Sally – whose husband was in prison for burglary – felt that support and sympathy for her or for the children were minimal: 'It was as if we had something contagious.'

On balance the message which came through was that a parent on his or her own, creating a new family, does feel very vulnerable. Society still does little to make room for a lone parent. The happiest men and women on their own seemed to be those who had reassembled the marital jigsaw into a fresh picture, and from them a positive attitude did shine through.

> JULIE: *'Don't forget to have fun. Coping alone with domestic chores and worrying about money can mean fun can go out of the window. Don't let it.'*

> DIANA: *'My kids are big fans of Barney and he has a great song about families. What the song basically says is that, "family is people and a family is love". It doesn't matter what your family consists of, just that you love each other. It is a great song for our situation.'*

> EDDIE: *'It is a blinkered view to see a family only in the couple plus 2.2 children. Families come in all shapes and sizes.'*

As we move forward in the following chapters to consider other alternatives of family life, we see that Eddie is right.

4   Stepparents

Millions of people are involved; millions more need to understand.

The National Stepfamily Association

Accepting the Situation

In the well-known fairy story, Snow White's mother dies when her daughter is born. A stepmother takes her place, a *wicked* stepmother. Later the stepmother feels threatened by Snow White's beauty and then she becomes jealous; competition for the father's attention sets the stepmother against her stepdaughter. The impact of this fable has been very damaging over the years to the social acceptance of stepfamilies. There is the Cinderella story too. Who hasn't been haunted by the picture of sad Cinders left to do the housework while her stepmother takes Cinderella's stepsisters to the ball?

Stepfamilies are in essence like any other family, but because they have to take into account previous relationships, they face specific challenges of their own. The very existence of a stepparent is a constant reminder of the breakdown and loss of an already established family group. A stepfamily does not start with a clean slate, and recognition must be given to the earlier family's dynamics. Success of the new stepfamily after a divorce may in the long run depend upon the care and attention which all those involved have paid to resolving the problems related to the breakup. Children need to have the situation explained in ways they can understand. No stepparent can just take on a parental role, and a stepparent needs to build, carefully and slowly, his or her own relationship with the child.

The first British study of children who have grown up in stepfamilies was published in 1998 (Barnes, Thompson, Daniel and Burchardt, 1998). One of the co-authors of the study, Gill Gorrell Barnes, a consultant at the Institute of Family Therapy, says her finding showed that three-quarters of the children interviewed said their natural parent did not explain what was happening to them at the time. This caused considerable distress, especially if they felt a parent was trying to deceive them. The researchers found that in many cases stepmothers were forced onto children with no real explanation from the natural father about what was happening. Therefore, the stepmother had a more difficult task from the beginning. On the other hand 'mothers usually introduced a stepfather slowly', and showed greater skills at introducing a new partner.

Families may find it difficult to acknowledge that they *are* a stepfamily. This may be because there is today still a 'second best' feeling about a stepfamily. Refusing to accept the situation may be linked to the adjectives frequently associated with stepfamilies – 'failure' and 'wicked' are two of them. And we must never forget that the prefix 'step' comes from an Old English word 'stoep' meaning bereavement. In an effort to hold the reality at bay, denial can be a form of protection, startling as this may seem.

> DEBORAH: *'Oh no, we're not a stepfamily – my children live with us and he only visits with his.'*

> JACK: *'My kids are grown up – so I guess not, really.'*

> GORDON: *'I'm an "out-of-step" parent I suppose. I am gay and together with my new partner we do care for three children full time.'*

If families are unclear about their status and what this means to all its members, there will be confusion, frustration, anger and hurt; inevitably, the conflicts will not be understood and so not untangled. A mistaken belief for all concerned can be that a new partner intends to take the role of a parent. Unless this is discussed and resolved, this can bring about resentment and recrimination. The Coordinator of Counselling for the National Stepfamily Association spoke to us about the problems the hopes of a parent can bring to the new family:

> CHERYL WALTERS: *'It is often the expectations of the parent when remarrying which cause difficulties. No one can join a family and take on half of everything. A new partner is not a new parent. The new partner needs time to build up a relationship with the child before being involved with the discipline.'*

Given the high rate of breakups for families first-time round, it is a daunting fact that a higher percentage of stepfamilies formed by remarriages, where it is the first marriage for one of the partners, eventually come to grief. As these failed marriages follow a prior divorce for at least one partner, the pain of a second or third family breakup is especially agonizing and long-lasting for children, parents, and the extended family. Earlier losses and insecurities are compounded.

'How do I get it right this time?' was the question that parents constantly asked themselves and us.

Importance of Timing

A popularly held belief is that after a wedding there is a continuing
honeymoon period during which the bride and groom dote on each
other as a couple prior to having a family, if in fact they want one.
Marrying someone who already has a family doesn't allow for that. If
you become a second wife to a man there is a good chance that he will
already have children. If you are the parent the children live with, it
can be a delicate decision how and when to introduce a 'friend' who
may become a partner.

> DEBORAH: *'When I met my husband, we had very few "proper
> dates" where we were alone. Our dates became family outings
> with his daughter as soon as things looked serious. In fact this
> summer we are planning our first holiday with just the two of us, it
> is to be our "honeymoon" after four-and-a-half years of marriage
> and two more children.'*

> VAL: *'After the dust of my divorce had settled I dated several men.
> Sometimes the relationship didn't develop and sometimes they
> progressed and lasted months. I didn't introduce any of them to my
> boys because I knew I didn't want to remarry yet, so I saw them all
> as temporary. This was the whole point, not permanent. I saw my
> men friends when the children were with their father or in bed. If I
> met a man that I hoped would be with me for a long time, then of
> course I would want him to meet my boys, for they are such a big
> part of my life.'*

> IVY: *'I knew I'd remarry one day, but not yet. However, I hadn't
> bargained on my son Bob (eleven years old). I dated Tony about four
> times, and each time he came he chatted for a while to my son about
> football.'*

What shocked and surprised Ivy was when she overheard Bob
telling a friend he now had 'a half-father in Tony because he was
keen on his Mum'. Ivy had, until then, not thought that the idea
of a possible stepfather had entered her boy's head. Ivy said she
became very self-conscious about her dates with Tony. She let
drop into the conversation that when and if she ever thought of
remarrying she would talk to Bob about it long before it
happened.

IVY: *'With the divorce, and disappearance of his dad, Bob had had quite enough shocks and changes. I went very slowly and carefully with Tony.'*

Belinda's children aged three and five were taken by their father and introduced to 'your new mother' without any preparation or warning.

BELINDA: *'When they came home they were incoherent with shock. Over the years it quietened down, but they have never ever accepted Catherine as their stepmum.'*

It is usual for a parent to be quite wary about introducing a work colleague or acquaintance to the children in case they read more into the situation than there is.

PHILIPPA: *'My sorrow is connected to a man whose wife left him with three little boys. We got to know each other at work and were certainly attracted to each other. We'd go out on dates but every time I suggested doing something with the children it would be vetoed. We split up in the end. It was so unreal.'*

This is a situation we heard about from other men and women. Yet, how do you know when to introduce a new 'friend', possibly a new partner, to the children? Too soon and it can be very painful for everyone if the relationship doesn't develop. Yet Philippa felt she was being kept away from the family, which seemed artificial and hurtful to her. Timing is all-important; a governing factor may be to protect the children, especially if they are still suffering from being left by a parent because of divorce or for any other reason.

JUDITH: *'I met Stephen after his wife had died. The boys were then fourteen and sixteen. They were still at school and I would have loved to have dashed in to look after them all. But Stephen was wise and we just saw each other for at least a year before I met the boys. It was another year before I moved in and by the time we married I believe we were already a family. Teenagers can be difficult and John and Rory were, but love between us all grew and the birth of our daughter brought joy to us all.'*

The Stepparent

> PHIL: *'I remarried, and Jenny and I thought she made a "good enough" stepmother to my nine- and seven-year-olds, while I remained their father. I found to my cost it's not so straightforward. If I make a stand and override either my ex-wife or Jenny over a decision about the children you can just feel the stress in the kids. On the other hand, if I just let them both get on with bringing up the children, I believe the kids feel abandoned. The strain on Jenny and me is unbelievable.'*

Phil's use of the expression 'good enough' echoes the findings of D.W. Winnicott, the psychoanalyst and paediatrician. He tried to reduce parental fears of failure by assuring parents that to be 'good enough' was just that, being 'good enough'. They did not have to aspire to perfection. Jenny, like countless other parents, wished she had had more forewarning about how to be a stepparent. She had not bargained on Phil's ex-wife being so conspicuous in their family life.

> PHIL, speaking about his new young wife: *'I don't think Jenny had any real idea of what she was getting into. We realize now that when becoming a stepparent you take on not just a new partner, and any children, but also the other parent.'*

Indeed, the first marriage may have been formally ended, but there are still strong family blood ties.

Being a stepparent is very hard and confusing at times. In spite of divorce and remarriage being so common today, people still shy away from talking about stepparenting or portraying it in the way it really is. Our earlier experiences may not provide us with ideas about how to act. Unless a clear framework can be established, it is all too easy to founder when searching for a new role within the new family. We heard often that 'instant parenthood is no joke!'

We were given many examples of parents embarking on a new relationship, with a child or children from an earlier relationship, with little more thought or preparation than a mental crossing of fingers. So many parents do not foresee difficulties ahead about not having a shared history, nor common ways of doing things. Families established for some time have a language made up of 'familiar' stories and jokes. An oblique reference to an event in the past will cause gales of happy laughter as a shared moment is recalled. A new family has to build a databank of these memories.

Many families learn, to their cost, that parents and stepparents are not interchangeable.

JUDE: *'I was so stupid – I married Tony and he had two boys from his marriage. I believed I should love them from the start. I didn't of course, and felt very guilty and the stress just mounted. I cried a lot.'*

TONY: *'What was so sad was that I knew Jude tried so hard – too hard I now realize. I didn't know how to help her.'*

Tony reinforced the belief that he had hoped all would be well, although he had been through a relationship where there had been difficulties centred around bringing up the children. Tony and his ex-wife could never agree on any aspect of childcare, yet he had still entered into another partnership hoping all would be well.

TONY: *'Good intentions are not enough – especially if you haven't understood what went wrong first time, and I found that out too late.'*

Reluctant Stepparent

Many people told us that a new partner is not always willing, or indeed able, to take on the responsibilities of a 'ready-made' family. We heard from Lorraine about her difficulties in becoming a stepmother:

LORRAINE: *'I fell in love with Andrew, but I was horrified at the thought of being a parent. I was too young and I didn't want a constant reminder that he had been married before. His daughter didn't like me either – so what was the point of us trying to play Happy Families?'*

BETH had similar worries: *'I wanted to marry Kevin. I did not want us to have a child together because I know relationships don't last in this day and age. So if you have a baby you are on your way to becoming a single parent at some time.'*

Beth continued her story by saying her attitude to children overall made it very hard for her to get involved with Kevin's daughters from his previous relationship.

SALLY: *'I, of course, am the wicked stepmother, and the children's mother is always on a pedestal.'*

JANICE: *'The first time I met Pauline she said to me, "Why did you steal Dad away from my mum?" We have never got on together.'*

JOYCE: *'I must admit to being a reluctant stepmum. I married George and he had a fifteen-year-old daughter. We didn't like each other really, and when a couple of years later George died unexpectedly, Maddy and I were left on our own. I told her "I'm all you've got, so you had better make the most of it. We didn't choose each other."'*

JEREMY: *'I truly love Ruth, but she has put her foot down about seeing my kids. She is not interested. I feel cut in half and can only hope that time alone will help her to change her mind. Meanwhile, I dread the choices I constantly have to make.'*

TERRY: *'She wants us to have a baby, but she can't even handle my children.'*

There is of course a fundamental difference between mothering and stepmothering and both take tremendous effort. Janey told us that if motherhood were as unfulfilling as stepmotherhood, then she didn't think she was up for it anyway. This is a situation which needs working through, for if she were to enter into a marriage with Bob hoping that a child by them together would be different and problem-free, it would result in greatly misplaced anger and resentment in later years.

GEORGE: *'I thought it might be fun to "play dad" and went quite happily to take my steady girlfriend out for the day with her kids. Never again – it was a nightmare. They tried to wind me up and were rude and, well, unpleasant. I couldn't understand how Julie could have such objectionable children. She seemed to think they were just fooling around and that things would get better. I didn't see it that way, and our relationship has definitely cooled.'*

From one woman we heard how her fantasy of being a stepmum did, indeed, end in tears:

BETH: *'I had seen the film "The Sound of Music" and when my new man told me he had four children from previous relationships,*

I imagined myself as Julie Andrews and the Von Trapp family. Me teaching them funny songs and getting them to love me. The reality was far from the dream. I went in the deep end. Jim took us all on a family holiday in a very remote cottage. I must have been mad to agree. I just couldn't cope with four children who didn't get on with each other all that well. I hadn't realized that there would be so much mess – and the cooking! If I tried to play, the food burnt or wasn't ready; if I cooked, there were no clean clothes. I suppose, if I had had a baby or even two of my own, I would have gradually got used to it all. As it was, they hated me, and I can't say I liked them very much. It's a pity, because I had such good intentions. I wish now I'd set out to be just friends with Jim's children. Julie Andrews has a lot to answer for.'

Beth had tried too hard and therefore found herself in very deep water. Perhaps as the children came from more than one relationship of her partner, she might have tried to get to know each individually, rather than take them all on at once in the artificial atmosphere of a family holiday. Time is needed to adjust – time to get to know one another. Growing to like somebody takes a while. And, of course, the more personalities involved, the greater the potential for anger and disruption.

SARAH understood Beth's optimism: *'My husband and I took on his two children shortly after getting married. They were a ten-year-old boy and an eleven-year-old girl. My goodness, the battles! I am still having trouble coping with these additions to my "perfect" life, but it seems to be getting better. The most difficult thing is the fact that I didn't have any underlying feelings of caring for these children, and when they did something negative, it only made it all worse.'*

MIRANDA: *'My stepson and I have had a love/hate relationship for three years. Sometimes he loves me and sometimes he hates me. When I stopped taking either situation personally and became indifferent to his tantrums of anger and manipulations and stopped playing into them, they disappeared.'*

Another woman we spoke to called herself a very reluctant step-mother: Alison met and married Brian, a widower who had a twelve-year-old daughter.

ALISON: *'Jackie and I didn't really talk to each other, we kept a respectful distance.'*

Events overtook this family with the sudden incapacitating illness of Brian after only one year of marriage.

ALISON: *'Jackie and I looked at each other across the hospital bed and I think we both had the same thought: "Oh God, what if I'm left with her?"'*

Fortunately, finance is not a problem for this family, and Jackie went to boarding school.

ALISON: *'I'll look after her physical needs, of course, but I can never be a loving mother to Jackie, although I love Brian. You can't love to order.'*

Taking on a Family

Very few people find it easy to take on a child or children of a new partner.

CAROL: *'My husband and I alone are a family. The boys' biggest goal is to break up our marriage. I thought we could have the loving family they didn't have with their mother because of her drug habit. Boy was I dead wrong. We are having to pay for the problems their mother caused. We have become the abused, and no one is listening.'*

ALICE: *'I didn't know how to handle Tom's two youngsters. Was I supposed to discipline them? I didn't know the rules. I decided to bide my time and watch and wait. I'm glad I did, because bit by bit I could see how the land lay and eventually feel I was on firm enough ground to correct them – mildly – when I felt they were out of order. I know Tom was very appreciative of the time and thought I gave the situation. I didn't rush at it and as Tom and I grew closer I could feel the children wanting to be included in our loving relationship.'*

SANDY tells a very different story: *'I knew Bill had a boy from his first marriage but he didn't talk about him much, and I didn't ask. Bill and I married, the week we got back, Bill's ex-wife turned up with Brian – a rebellious fifteen-year-old who had just been excluded from school. Bill took him in as he said he now had a family life to offer Brian. I remember saying "Who me? A mother? Oh no!" But it was oh yes, as far as Bill and his ex were concerned. Brian was trouble from the word go. Bill and I never had a chance and I left him six months later.'*

Sandy and Bill, unlike Alice and Tom, rushed in, where indeed angels fear to tread. There seems to have been no time given to thinking through the situation, weighing up the pros and cons and working out the best timing. Sandy and Bill had not had a long enough spell together as a couple. They had known each other only three months before they married and, as Sandy reported, the situation regarding Bill's son was not discussed.

SANDY: *'I didn't want to ask or know much about Brian and I was right. When he did come into our lives, it spoilt everything.'*

BILL talked with us too: *'I always felt bad about leaving Sarah and my son. I suppose I took it for granted that when I remarried I would do my share and give him a home. He was a handful and I feel guilty that it is because I left when he was ten. It wasn't fair to Sandy, though. But she could have tried harder.'*

SUZY: *'I was out of my depth. Colin said we would be all right and I believed him. But on a practical level it was awful. His kids were rude to me and one day I smacked his little boy. I didn't know what else to do. The balloon went up and his mother was furious – later Colin and I had a dreadful row. It wasn't that I was a wicked stepmother, just a very scared twenty-five-year-old. That incident created a terrible atmosphere for weeks.'*

JUNE: *'Years after I had failed as a stepmother I realized that a stepmum is not supposed to replace a real mum. It's different and could take years to settle into a loving relationship. I didn't know that at the time and tried to blot out my husband's ex-partner. Actually, he is also now my ex.'*

It is tragic that June discovered, too late, that the memories and relationships from the first family cannot, and should not, be taken away or erased. All too frequently we heard, 'I fell in love, and thought it would all work out. The children had other agendas.'

The Other Parent

There is another important factor to take into account: when marrying the person you love, who already has children, the other parent must be considered.

BETTY: '*I acquired my stepkids at ages ten and thirteen. They lived with us for that tough adolescence time and it was as if someone had stuck a couple of aliens into my sitting room. It was so difficult. Then of course you have the ex-wife in the background. Never, never forget the ex. If there are children, the ex will be around forever, I suppose.*'

TONY: '*I fully accepted I was marrying a woman with three children. What I found difficult was her ex – or the children's father if you like – often hanging around. Pete would bring the boys back from his weekend and expect a drink and a chat before he left. He seemed to think it was his right, and seemed at home. I was uncomfortable about it but felt it was churlish to make a fuss.*'

Tony's wife, Anita, felt quite comfortable about Pete staying around the house. Having him there seemed natural to her and 'the children liked it'. Anita had not been aware that Tony had strong feelings about this, but once it was in the open she called a halt to Pete's casual attitude and expectations of a welcome. Was Pete right?

ANDREW disagreed strongly: '*When I became the stepfather of Richard and Nigel I made it clear this was our home now. Okay, their Dad used to live here, but that's in the past and I certainly would not ever have made their father welcome.*'

Andrew's wife, Pam, told us that whenever her ex-partner arrived to collect the children there was always a bad atmosphere which frequently ended in a row between Andrew and Pam. In our previous book *Where's Daddy?* we discussed at length the disturbing effect upon children and parents at hand-over time. We now see that where stepparents are involved, they, too, do not find this an easy path to navigate.

JOANNA: '*I cannot believe I still have such strong feelings about my husband's first wife three years after they divorced. I have never thought of myself as a jealous person, but I suppose I am. John goes off to collect the kids from her and I am really on edge until he gets back. I go wild if I think he has had a cup of tea with her.*'

Yet there can be a more positive view of the ex-partner of a husband:

JOYCE: '*Bill left me to go to Mary. They had a daughter – then he left them to marry Sally and they have a son. The funny thing is*

Mary and I have grown to like each other and now Mary and her little girl come on holiday with me and my new family. It may look like a muddle from the outside, but Mary and I feel we have a lot in common – we both pity Sally.'

What can be unsettling for the new family is the break when some children leave to spend time with their non-resident parent. The interruption of a growing routine can cause tensions and in itself take time to get used to. It can be unsettling, too, for the children of a subsequent marriage to see their stepsiblings go away for treats and extra holidays.

MILLY: *'It can upset the balance of our family quite dramatically when my fourteen-year-old goes off with his dad for a skiing holiday. My ten- and nine-year-olds feel really put out, and it makes it hard for Tom to settle back with us and for us to be a family again. Real families share experiences.'*

For a child who only 'visits' a family, keeping a balance is hard. 'Fairness' is a quality children in stepfamilies were quick to watch out for, always on guard to see if there is a favourite.

SUE: *'We'd be fine and settled and then two teenagers would arrive, looking for trouble, I thought. My heart went out to "our" two who were much younger, didn't really understand, but had to move over for Dad's other children.'*

BEN (Sue's husband): *'I would try to make my two welcome, but I could see the effect it had on the little ones. It always felt awful – damned if I made the time special, and damned if I didn't.'*

Blended Families

Being a brother or sister is not always easy, even in established families, and when adolescents are struggling to find autonomy it is at times especially difficult for a stepfamily to keep this in mind. Add to this the mixture of stepchildren and half-siblings and the situation becomes even more complicated. The National Stepfamily Association advised:

CHERYL WALTERS: *'There must be house rules for all the children, visiting and non-resident. They need to be aware of the same rules. The parent dishes out the discipline, supported by the partner.'*

BERYL remembers what it was like to be the only stepchild: *'I watched my stepmum like a hawk to see if she gave my little brother more of anything. Looking back she was very good, but I know I gave her and my Dad a lot of grief.'*

NIGEL: *'"Blended?" Well, two of hers, two of mine and one of ours. I'd call it more like scrambled.'*

KIM: *'It wasn't until Dave and I had our own baby that I felt we were a family. Of course that included Dave's six-year-old, it was then we all just merged together. I felt more confident I suppose?'*

NICK: *'My stepson is bloody rude to me. I can cope, but I see red when he picks on my two boys who are younger.'*

GEOFF: *'The children from my first marriage are at the same school as my new wife's children. They don't really get on – even though we do combine holidays. I have felt odd when meeting my stepchildren from school and just waving to my own kids. At school events we all keep our distance. My ex doesn't like to mix.'*

DIANA: *'I love my stepson who is ten. Yet it is so different to have your own baby totally dependent on you. No visitation, no shared weekends. Someone to call you Mummy, not Di. Here is a child who will have a history with you. Most importantly as your own child reaches the tumultuous adolescent time, there will be an existing relationship to fall back on during times of anger.'*

For Graham and Maggie a large blended family does work and they manage somehow to give each child some individual space and for them all to combine at times into one large family.

GRAHAM: *'I love the fact of mine, yours, and ours. We all go camping and I laugh when I see people trying to work out our relationship. Seven kids under ten years!'*

MAGGIE: *'Space is very important. Graham's girls visit a lot, and I make sure they have a locked cupboard where they can keep their own things safe – they know they won't be touched until they next come to us. I couldn't bear to see them arrive with a little case each time with a toothbrush. They are not visitors.'*

Who Will Call me Mum?

Women can feel 'out of it' in several ways. To be without a child of your own, yet being a part-time stepparent can be unsettling.

> CHRISTINE: *'I long for a child of my own. My "steps" call me Chrissy and I know they would never call me Mum. I wouldn't want them to. I don't take the place of their Mum. I'm an extra. But I would like to be somebody's real Mum ...'*

> MAVIS: *'Two out of three stepchildren call me Mummy, their choice, not mine. I still feel very uncomfortable about it.'*

> MARIE: *'We have his kids for the holidays – the focus is on them – we as a couple get lost in the process.'*

> LAURA: *'I know we will never have a child of our own. He has had a vasectomy.'*

> POLLY: *'I long for a child – yet my husband has five. At forty the last thing he wants is to start with nappies and bottles again.'*

Both women and men spoke about their partners with children who are reluctant to have a further child – even if the new relationship is felt to be strong and secure.

> ROB: *'My first marriage went wrong when the babies began to arrive. We went on having more to keep us from focusing on the problems in the marriage itself. I guess I am not making the same mistakes again.'*

A constant theme was that children cause a strain on a relationship. Yet Rob tells us he and his ex-wife had children to keep them distracted from problems within the marriage. How does Rob deal with any difficulties that arise in his new relationship with Penny? He is adamant he will not have any more children and will face difficulties head on.

On the other side of the picture is Bill:

> BILL: *'I long to have a child together with my new wife, Sue, but she says her experience of being a stepmother to my boys has put her off the idea of motherhood.'*

Sue seems to find it hard to believe things will be different with her own baby. She will have a shared history and memories with her baby from the beginning. Also, she will not have the stress of disrupted weekends and family turmoil. There will be no 'other' parent in the background.

> JACK: 'I won't have a child with my second wife. It would cause problems for my children from my first marriage. They would feel very jealous because our child would live with me and they don't.'

Jack's first marriage casts a shadow over his present relationship. He is unable to feel entirely free with his second wife because of his anxiety about his children.

Finding a Path Through the Minefield

Of course, we heard from stepfamilies where the transition from one family to another had gone smoothly:

> PETER: 'I love my stepchildren, but I am not their father, and they do remind me of this at times of anger. When we get along well, we get on really well and when we don't, we really don't. But this could be said of my own children when they get to be this age.'

> SEAN: 'I just want to say that raising a child is tough whether it is yours or someone else's, so please keep an open mind as it's all too easy to walk away and blame it on the new family situation.'

> LAURA: 'I had a broken marriage behind me when I met Alan – who had two sons of fourteen and seventeen. His wife had died, so I suppose it is fair to say we both had our share of pain. We both needed time to grieve over loss and we got to know each other slowly. I didn't meet the boys for over a year but once we knew we wanted to marry we talked and talked. We talked over every detail and tried to look at what it would mean for all four of us.'

Laura went on to describe, vividly, the way they discussed possible areas of conflict – jealousy and envy were two likely danger spots. Laura knew herself well enough to anticipate there would be times when she would have to come second in Alan's life and because of her own vulnerability after her divorce she was concerned about how she would manage this. The boys, too, were still reacting from the shock of their mother's death and there were strong feelings (both good and bad) about Laura joining the family. By the time they married all four were ready to combine as a family.

LAURA: *'The wedding was a very important ritual for us. We were supported by the love and help from both our parents plus the parents of Alan's first wife. Two years later when a daughter was born, it truly completed our family.'*

JACK also spoke of the more positive side: *'I fell in love with Annie who has two children. When I knew I wanted to marry Annie I knew by then I wanted to take on the whole family. Before we reached that point we went through several stages of indecision and planning. If I had to sum it up, I would say to anyone, go slow, very slow and don't take anything for granted. It's a big decision to take on a family and you're only asking for trouble if you believe you are marrying a woman plus her kids. I knew I was marrying the woman I loved plus two other people I was growing to love and believed they were starting to feel affection for me. It didn't happen overnight – I had to earn their love and respect. For a dad that's a given, but a stepdad has to work at it. Believe me.'*

AUDREY: *'I got in touch with the Stepfamily Association. I urge any stepparent to do that. After all, other parents can advise you about possible minefields. As the saying goes, "it's good to talk". They can also give advice on practical matters, and there is a Helpline if you really need someone to talk to.'*

The National Stepfamily Association has a list of information sheets, and they work with the media, professionals in statutory and voluntary agencies, and lobby politicians to ensure that legislation reflects the needs of stepparents. One statistic should be highlighted – if it were more widely known it would have prevented much of the heartache reported to us – 'It takes between two and ten years for a stepfamily to settle.' One cause of stress can be that a child may try to come between the new couple. This may be tolerated more easily if it is understood. As Cheryl Walters told us, 'The child is saying can I trust you to stay, and not to leave me like my mum/dad did?' The strength of the family is being tested.

Those who were most stressed agreed they had not thought enough about how complicated it can be. To imagine one can fit into a natural parent's shoes without difficulty is at best naive, and at worst foolhardy. Even if everybody involved is in agreement, toes can be trodden on and feelings hurt. It takes time to build family memories made up of events and shared experiences.

> NANCY: *'I remind myself a dozen times a day that kids are kids and in any family the path is often stony and uphill. After all it's just that as a stepmother I feel I do have to try that bit harder all the time. I don't even love my own children all the time.'*

Graham passed on a tip that all the adults need to communicate about parenting strategies. He felt it was unfair to raise children in homes with different sets of rules.

> CAROL: *'At first I only thought about how Bob and I should make a family with his children. With difficulty as it turned out. But, I began to think what it had all meant for the children and once I saw it through their eyes I had much more sympathy and patience.'*

The expectations of a stepmother do seem greater than those of a stepfather. She is responsible for the day-to-day care in the home. She is, after all, at the heart of the family. A merged family starts out with a complicated agenda. The reasons for the breakup of the original family and the way the change was handled with the children have a major bearing on the way the stepfamily settles down. Dealing with children's questions, explanations and reassurances are a must if the pathway is to be successfully negotiated. The children may have witnessed rows, arguments and violence, so this will have an influence on the way they view their new family. As Gill Gorell Barnes (1998) found: 'The family difficulties did not begin with the divorce but preceded it.' In addition the experiences of the children will have left an indelible mark and will affect their relationship with the new stepparent, just as in the future with their choice of a partner.

> LUCY: *'I received a postcard from my father: "Guess what, I'm on my honeymoon!" I never liked Maria. My brother and I used to call her boot-face.'*

What chance did this stepmother have?

The message to all men and women creating a merged family seems to be not to expect too much too soon, either from themselves or from the other family members. There will be a transition period, almost certainly lasting for years, when different needs have to be balanced. But by recognizing that stepfamily life is stressful and demanding and by seeking help if it is needed, families can and do move on to mobilize the family strength.

A final word from D.W. Winnicott (1955 (1993)): 'A correspondent asked for a meeting of unsuccessful stepparents. I think such a meeting would be fruitful. It would be composed of ordinary men and women.'

5   Lesbian and Gay Parents

The bond that links your true family is not one of blood, but of respect and joy in each other's life.

Richard Bach

Same-sex Partners

What makes a good parent? Love and care of a child. Nevertheless, these qualities are not necessarily seen as compatible with the choice of a partner, especially if the partner is of the same sex. In the United Kingdom there are no firm figures about how many children are raised in a family where one or both parents are homosexual, but in the United States at the present time at least six million children are being cared for by couples of the same sex.

Lesbian mothers and gay fathers still face great prejudice in the courts, both in the United Kingdom and the United States, if they are in dispute with their former spouses over custody or contact arrangements. In addition, lesbian and gay co-parents are not recognized in law. The child has no legal right to have his or her relationship with the co-partner recognized, no right to inherit if the co-parent dies intestate and no right to maintenance if the couple splits up.

'Coming out' as a gay person nearly always means a disruption of family life and the ensuing relationships. Even today it is not unusual for family, colleagues and friends to be shocked and perhaps less than understanding.

LARRY: 'I "came out" one year ago, but it has been so hard I am thinking of going back in again.'

To be a single gay person is one thing and there are now clubs, magazines, meetings and a network of support, where new friends can be found. To be a parent 'coming out' is a much more complicated situation. In addition to parents and friends, there are a partner and children to be told about this fundamental change.

DEBBIE: 'The fear of people's opinion and losing my kids has been the single biggest thing that has kept me in denial. It took years for me to come to a deeper understanding about myself. It is as if I

*have finally found some secret information about myself, but you
do hear some awful court cases where lesbian mums have lost
custody of their children.'*

We were often told of the isolation gay parents can feel, especially at
the sensitive moment of deciding whether or not to tell those closest
about this drastic change in life. Still today, there are stereotyped ideas
about gays, about the way they behave, talk and dress. Everyone has an
opinion about whether or not a homosexual should parent a child.

When a woman or a man comes out, she or he always has a
huge hurdle to overcome to make public this private decision. Who
to tell first? The perspectives differ for parents, partners and
children. It is an overwhelming fact that there is very little support
– emotional or otherwise – for any lesbian or gay parent. So how
and when to tell? Do you decide to tell your partner first, or your
children or both your parents? Together or separately? How do you
know the 'right' time to tell?

Parents' Reactions

Many people we interviewed told their parents first in the hope of
acceptance and support.

> LAWRENCE: *'I "came out" after ten years of marriage. Neither my
> parents nor my wife could come to terms with what I was saying. I
> had no idea they would be so homophobic. I never see my kids.
> What on earth has a person's sexual orientation got to do with
> parenting skills?'*

Not all parents react in a negative way, although not surprisingly
nearly all mothers and fathers do need time to make the necessary
adjustments to the news. They may be totally unprepared. Lawrence
said his father, in bewilderment, blurted out, 'But you have got
children', while his mother cried, and asked if he had AIDS.

> CHRISTINE: *'I never could find the right time – so I picked a time
> when my mum couldn't get away from me. We were driving in a
> car on an eight-hour trip. I told her about halfway home. She took it
> pretty well.'*

> BRIAN: *'Our son wrote to us along these lines. "I am gay – not your
> fault or mine, its just life!" He went on to say he hated any lies*

between us and wanted to share his new life and family with us. Molly and I had a lot of talking to do. She had to give up the idea of grandchildren and a daughter-in-law to fuss over, for a start. But we still had a family, even if it were not the one we had hoped for.'

Yet parents can sometimes find they are looked upon as failures because their child is gay.

HESTER: *'My daughter is a lesbian and my mother asked me where I thought I'd gone wrong in her upbringing.'*

JENNY: *'As parents, my husband and I still feel guilty and responsible. We both worry is it our fault Sally is gay?'*

OLIVE: *'My husband "outed" me. That really caused a problem for my parents and our kids.'*

Olive told us of the dreadful experience when her husband shouted out his suspicions at a family function. Olive went on to tell us she didn't know whether to comfort her children, her parents or to deal with her own shock of betrayal. Her parents were unable to accept their daughter's feelings.

A mother who met with us said it took years for her to accept that a child of hers was homosexual. She felt she had lost her only child. It took a very long time for her to let go of her feelings of sadness, guilt, and a sense of failure. 'I had to be re-educated,' she said.

ANGELA: *'I found out my son was gay at the same time as being told he had AIDS. If only I had known earlier. Those last few years could have been so different. We had lost touch. My husband and I thought we had no family, but we had a loved son too frightened to tell us who he really was. What kind of parents does that make us?'*

DIANE: *'The main problem for me is having to bite my tongue when I hear ignorant, hurtful remarks about gays. I am happy that my family includes my gay son and his partner.'*

PENNY: *'I couldn't get a grip when my son first told me he was gay and HIV positive. Acceptance was a lifeline. I had someone to talk to without fear of rejection or prejudice.'*

Acceptance is a helpline and support group for parents of lesbians and gay men. A newsletter encourages parents to share their experiences both good and bad, after being told that their child is gay. Through Acceptance we spoke to Susan. She very much wanted to talk and to be heard, to help to break down the wall of secrecy.

> SUSAN: *'I have been through it. When my son who was fourteen told me he thought he was gay I didn't know what to say. I had to come to understand it. I had no help, my husband did not understand, and neither did my vicar. I felt so alone. I rang Acceptance and said, "Please help me" and they did.'*

Susan, like many parents, looks back at the time before being told and says it hurts that it took so long for her son to be able to tell her he is gay. Advice from Susan to any parent is, 'Take a deep breath, before you say anything. It is only too easy to say "no!"or "I can't cope with this." What your son or daughter needs to hear is, "I'm your Mum and I love you."'

Pam also said her husband's reaction was to reject their son, and he has never wavered. He refuses to meet their son and his partner.

> PAM: *'I feel so alone – even my son has his partner to talk to. We could so easily open our hearts and be a new family.'*

Audrey, too, felt caught between her son and her husband:

> AUDREY: *'When my son told me he is gay he begged me not to tell his father. I haven't, but it puts a great strain on me.'*

> SUSAN: *'I can't see what the fuss is about, and I tell that to other parents. What makes a family? Love. Jesus gave us one thing, love – can't we give it out to others without conditions?'*

Another organization, Families and Friends of Lesbian and Gays, has a very useful informative leaflet on 'Telling Your Parent'. While acknowledging that all families are different it gives helpful guidelines. One important piece of advice is that you should try to help a concerned parent see that being lesbian or gay is not just a matter of sex, but that love, happiness, trust and affection with a partner are still possible, but with someone of your own sex.

The Stonewall Parenting Group meets monthly in London to offer mutual support and to campaign on the behalf of gay parents. Happy Families is another organization which started in 1995 when a need was identified for a self-help group for gay, lesbian and bisexual parents and their children. Its aim is to strengthen the family bonds that already exist. It also helps parents with the task of 'coming out' to their children and family. Not an easy thing to do, even in the late 1990s.

Glyn and Richard are the co-founders of Happy Families. They told us:

> 'The support for our type of family is growing and ever stronger in numbers. Together we have a brighter future, but we must all stop hiding and stand up and be counted. Only two years ago I was a closet parent, now I don't care. It's their problem if they don't like me and what I stand for.'

From their contacts with other members of Happy Families they believe that children of gay and lesbian people are more open-minded and are less prejudiced than children brought up in homes where myths and misconceptions about homosexuality abound.

> MARGE in Scotland: 'My neighbours made my life a misery – they would call out after me "filthy dyke". At school they would call my eldest son a queer – I had no one to talk to. Thank God for Happy Families. I had no other family.'

The Partner Left Behind

How can one find the words to tell a partner that something taken for granted – sexual love and desire – no longer exists? In many cases there is a dawning realization that it had never truly been there.

> LAURIE: 'It was all a big mistake – I should never have married. How do you say these words? I choked over them for months before I finally told my now ex-wife.'

> MEGAN: 'I made it worse by telling my husband I loved him still, but only like a sister. He has never forgiven me for my "deceit" as he calls it.'

> BARBARA: 'My husband left me after many years of marriage and several children. We had what I thought was a good marriage. Then there was the hell of discovery, grief, deceit, anger and more anger. At first my husband blamed God – and then decided it was my fault he had to decide between two lifestyles.'

Barbara, in common with other women, felt her husband had the easier option, because it was his choice and his beliefs he was following. Dave came out of the closet, but how was the family to come out of their own closet of secrecy? The family's life was turned upside down. The issue that caused the most trouble was in reality the least important: what will the neighbours think? Homophobia does not only affect an openly gay person, but sometimes straight family members can find themselves ostracised or viewed with suspicion.

> PAULINE: *'My husband left us to live a completely new life, but he forbade me to tell the children he thought he was gay.'*

Pauline was very uncertain what to do or what to say. On one hand her family life as she had known it was shattered. Yet she felt unwilling to broadcast the news of her husband's uncertainty. What if he decided he wasn't gay? Would he then return? What if she had already told the family of his dilemma? To suffer alone was hard, but until Brian made a final decision Pauline felt she had no option but to keep silent and fend off the questions from parents and family. Pauline and Brian had two adolescent boys and a little girl of six. Both boys became very difficult at home: two previously cooperative sons became morose and their school work suffered. Eileen began to wet her bed and to regress to 'baby-talk'; all of which added to Pauline's troubles.

> PAULINE: *'Sometimes I thought I would just blurt out "your father's gay" and leave them to get on with it. Then I'd stop and think it wasn't fair on Brian. It was his secret, not mine.'*

Very often we heard of the partners left behind feeling confused and sometimes foolish because of being part of a pretence. Sometimes they were unaware of the facts and they did not suspect that anything was wrong with the sexual side of their marriage.

> BARBARA: *'I sometimes feel my husband is getting away with murder, the murder of our family and our dreams and our future.'*

When a couple separates, the parent left behind with the children always experiences a host of difficulties. Self-esteem reaches a low point, and being rejected for another partner deeply affects most spouses. Where the choice of a 'significant other' also brings about the added complication of sexual preference, the shock is likely to be greater. 'I really didn't know' and 'I feel so stupid' and 'I feel betrayed' and sometimes 'I feel I have to doubt my own sexuality now' were the most frequent comments.

GEORGE: *'I know I would have been shattered anyway by Myrna leaving, but for her to go off with a girlfriend left me totally bewildered and bereft. Why hadn't I guessed? I didn't know who to talk to. I tried to tell my doctor, but he got embarrassed.'*

RAY: *'After eleven years of marriage we hit a bad patch. In the end, in exasperation, I asked my wife if she might be gay. She said she thought she was. I felt physically ill and was off work for a month. I rang around everywhere to find someone to talk to. In the end I found Parent's Friend and they just let me talk for hours. They asked me if I though Pat might be bisexual and that gave me hope we might continue together, but she wasn't. I know now it was nobody's fault. I have turned out to be more tolerant than I thought I was, and that must be good.'*

Judy said that after seven years of marriage she began to notice many changes in her husband Jack:

JUDY: *'Actually he became more like the man I fell in love with and who had slowly disappeared over the years.'*

The description which followed told us about a more carefree, light-hearted man about the house. The atmosphere in the home which had become leaden became easier. Judy began to relax, and the children were calmer and happy.

JUDY: *'I began to think that we were a truly close and loving family again. Even sex was good.'*

For Judy, this made the blow, when it came, harder to understand. Jack told her clearly, without any buildup or warning, that he had fallen in love, and hoped Judy could see her way to being happy for him as 'it had nothing to do with her'. A stunned Judy could hardly take in what Jack was saying with such enthusiasm and excitement. Jack now knew he was gay, and had become involved with a man he met at a club. He had, he repeated, fallen in love.

JUDY: *'I had no idea whatsoever that he had even been out socially without me.'*

It was very hard for Jack to understand why Judy could not 'take in' all he was saying, and be happy for him.

JUDY: *'It was as if he was speaking a foreign language. He gave no thought to my pain and he did not need to mourn the loss of what we had had together.'*

The realization for Jack that he was gay, and the acceptance of this by both him and his new friends had liberated him to such a degree that he lost sight of the shattered family around him. This does indicate something of the pressure that Jack must have felt for years, if the relief in 'coming out' meant that he could not see the grief and shock that this caused for his wife and children.

JUDY: *'Jack was so happy even I could see that, and at times felt such a surge of love for this dear man, then rage and pain at losing him.'*

It took years, and hours of psychotherapy, Judy told us, before she could feel that Jack was right when he said it had nothing to do with her. It was about Jack and his sexuality; in a way he had to follow his instincts and be who he is.

JUDY continued: *'I wish Jack had "come out" slowly and quietly. Instead he "burst out" and I was left fumbling in the dark with no idea how to cope or what to tell the kids. Actually Jack did that and I think told them in such a positive light, with such enthusiasm, they seem okay about the gay part. They did, of course, hate the way our family split up. I felt I needed therapy, not because of Jack, but to look at myself and to question why I married Jack in the first place. I still love him, you see.'*

Karen spoke of the love her ex-husband still feels for her.

KAREN: *'I love Sally now. My husband and I are in the process of separating and he has been wonderfully supportive of my decision. We are both totally committed to our son, and we will always be friends, probably best friends. He is a wonderful father and a wonderful person. He is helping me to make the transition to a new life. I believe this will help lessen the overall adjustment for our son and me.'*

ANGELA: *'I felt like dying inside, yet I felt I had a duty to help my husband keep a strong bond with the children. He is after all still their father.'*

In the United States, there is a network of support groups for straight spouses of gay partners. But this kind of help does not appear to be readily available yet in the United Kingdom.

ANNIE: *'My husband has just told me he is gay. He has found a support group to talk to. I have no one. I am on Prozac now. I love him still, but of course, something about our intimate life has died.'*

Annie says they cannot tell either of their parents, and because they go to fewer family gatherings, this is splitting the extended family. She feels they cannot take the risk of telling them, especially Jack's parents. Jack's brother had many years ago told them he thought he was gay and 'they beat it out of him'. She has told their ten-year-old daughter, but not yet the five-year-old. 'I don't have the language', said Annie.

Yet from Kate we hear of the way she and her husband have managed their situation:

KATE: *'I was pregnant with my first child when I married George. Later I was to hear that he had decided to have sex before marriage to see if he could manage it – that he always did wonder if he were a homosexual. We had three more children, and it was fifteen years later he told me he was in love with a friend of ours. Look at it this way: we had so much in common apart from the children that I decided that so long as he continued to love me, I shouldn't get too fussed that he loved someone else too. He goes on holiday with his friend, I hate the word "lover", but we have a good family life. We have told three of the children, now all in their thirties, but not our youngest child.'*

We asked why this should be so? George replied:

GEORGE: *'Angela is married to a very rigid young man. I believe if we told her, they might stop us seeing our grandchildren, and I couldn't bear that.'*

Kate had been in touch with Parent's Friend to talk to them, not for support for herself, but in a belief that she could help other men or women who find they are married to someone who is struggling with his or her sexual identity. She now counsels others, and finds that the most frequent questions are about how to tell children, and when and what to tell family and friends. What causes her concern is that each person she speaks with feels alone and that there seems to be no way of getting guidance about the way to handle this family dilemma.

> KATE: *'I haven't been left behind by George. It is just something that life has thrown up. I wasn't expecting twins, but I had them. I wasn't expecting George to be gay. My greatest concern has been to help him, not to blame him. I love him, and I know he still loves me.'*

Kate and George have also decided not to tell their brothers and sisters, but this decision has been made jointly.

For a wife or husband left behind it can be a cruel experience to have to deal with the loss and anger, especially if the decision is made not to tell family and friends the cause of the breakup. Talking to someone who can help you understand what your partner has had to deal with, or reading around the subject can make the whole situation more bearable, but getting access to assistance of this kind is not always easy.

Putting yourself in the shoes of your ex-partner makes it a little easier to understand the stress of attempting to deny one's homosexuality. However, a helpline, therapy or counselling, and books can help. Time will be needed to recover from the pain as you mourn the death of a relationship you thought you had.

Gay Families

Families headed by two gay men or two lesbian women are generally little understood, and so not all gay couples will make their lifestyle known. According to Stonewall, an organization dedicated to supporting lesbian and gay parents, one of the most insidious myths about lesbians and gay men is that they cannot and should not have children. In fact, they can and they do. Some have children before realizing they are gay; others come out first and then decide to have children, either by insemination or by finding a donor. Some take on the parenting role when they become the partner of someone who already has children.

> DON: *'People we chose to tell about our situation are very supportive. Probably our self-protective reflexes act as radar.'*

Don and his partner, both in their forties, live together. He has two sons from his marriage.

DON: *'When I told my eldest boy I was gay he replied, "Now I can understand the reasons for your unhappiness. I thought it was me you were unhappy with."'*

Don and his boyfriend would very much like to belong to a support group for gay fathers. He has friends and they all report that any hostility they have received from people at large is usually connected with the breakup of the marriage rather than because they are gay.

DON: *'The other parent can have a substantial effect on whether the child adjusts quickly. The gay issue is only a part of it all.'*

Some gay fathers in the United States spoke to us of their relief at no longer having to keep any secrets about what they are from those they love; and how much they gained from being able to share experiences, and to support each other in an often hostile world.

BEN, in New York: *'I am gay and knowing that and learning to live with it has made my kids more tolerant and open-minded. I do believe that kids need a mother and father, but who says they have to live and love together?'*

LOUISE, in the United Kingdom: *'I grew up in a pretty standard home – Mum, Dad, two sisters and myself. I was always taught or maybe brainwashed that this was the way things were meant to be. Later my sister Kate "came out" as a lesbian after a divorce and two children. She has a girlfriend, Annie, and the kids love her too. Sixteen years on they are still one happy family all living together.'*

Not every story has a happy ending and parents can lose their children because of their sexuality. One stereotypical view is that lesbians and gay men do not form meaningful relationships with each other. This can cause real difficulties for the families concerned.

NED: *'I told my wife, and she was off. I did see my kids for a bit, but the strain on all of us was too much. Even my own parents thought I shouldn't see them because I am now a homosexual.'*

From the replies we received, it was evident that Ned's parents' attitude is, sadly, fairly typical.

NED: *'I think my parents would have been okay with my being gay but they couldn't take my contact with the children.'*

Another misconception held by some is that all lesbian/gay people want to have a sexual relationship with a child. It is one of those ugly myths that have grown up in society, and distort the general view of homosexuality. It is very hard to have to choose between the desire to be authentic and honest, and the fear that by doing so, harm, pain and confusion will be caused to those you love. However, the anguish of having a relationship where you feel you are living a fabrication has to be faced. It can feel as if you are 'damaging your soul':

MELANIE: 'It took the death of a close friend to make me think about my life. You only get one shot at it. I took the plunge. I have two sons who now live with my partner and me, although they started out with their father. I was very anxious at the beginning about custody.'

LAURA: 'After eight years of marriage and three wonderful kids I decided I needed to live my life and not the life that made everyone else happy. It had begun by being the perfect daughter, good wife and mother. Exit husband, hello freedom. Kids are still wonderful, and I met a Princess Charming.'

CONNIE: 'I've been out with my little girl and local lads have shouted at me that they ought to rape me to straighten me out. Thank God Sandy is only three. I am terrified my ex-partner will try to take her away.'

Connie has met the aggression which can stalk any homosexual.

JUNE: 'I hope my daughter is straight. I wouldn't want her to go through what I've been through by being a lesbian.'

RUBY: 'I haven't had problems with custody. My ex doesn't pay child maintenance, and his nineteen-year-old girlfriend is due to give birth to his child next week. My mum and mum-in-law both feel they have done their job as far as child raising goes, so they don't interfere. I live with Linda, and the children like their co-mum a lot and we're doing fine.'

We asked Ruby and Linda if they encountered prejudice because of their family situation:

RUBY: 'Seldom anything open. People almost always assume my older child is mine and the youngest are my co-mum's and that we are just friends.'

There does not seem to be prejudice or a problem with those friends and neighbours who do guess the real nature of the relationship. Ruby thinks it's because 'those who do work it out may be more likely to have gay and lesbian friends and be more open-minded. On the whole people don't see what they don't want to see.'

> GORDON: 'My son was nine when I told him I was gay. It was on the day after I told him that his mother and I were getting divorced which totally surprised him. I felt compelled to tell him I was gay to help him understand the reason for the divorce. What really surprised me was his response. He said, "So?" I then asked him if he understood what it meant? His reply was "Yeah! That means you love boys and not girls." Never underestimate a nine-year-old.'

Gordon continued by telling us that whereas his sexuality had not become an issue between him and his son, what did distress Jimmy was the battle that ensued over custody. 'That has affected him.'

Family, friends and neighbours can be kind and understanding, but some will keep their distance because they will not know what to say or how to act:

> KATIE: 'I have had it said to my face, "If you raise your son on your own he will be gay too." Well, my parents are heterosexual and they raised me to be heterosexual, but I'm not, so why should my son be gay? He will be whatever he is, and I will love him for that.'

Children's Attitudes to Lesbian and Gay Parents

Same-sex couples are often faced with the extra burden of how to tell the children and how to behave in front of them. 'Should we pull apart when my son enters the room?', asked Lily. 'Should we define our relationship to my teenager?', worried Marilyn. Lesbian couples were faced by a variety of reactions from their children: 'You are a mother, and mothers don't have sex lives, do they?', Jenny was told by her daughter; and from Alice: 'This issue with my kids scares me to death. I don't mind if I lose my family over my relationship with my partner, but the kids are a more delicate issue and can't be lost.'

> SALLY: 'I told Colin last summer, when he was fourteen, that I am gay, and of the type of relationship Ruthie and I have. He said he already knew. He told me that he did not have a problem having a gay mum.'

Sally, like countless other lesbian mothers, says that her child does not have a problem with the relationship. Also in common with other lesbian mothers and gay fathers, Sally says her child finds it difficult to comprehend why people talk in such an antagonistic way about gay people. We heard of children being defensive and indignant when reading or hearing something negative about gay couples. Another thread which emerged was that although many children are made to understand that their parent is not ashamed of being a homosexual, and is proud of the family, the family situation is nevertheless not something to talk about to everyone. The problem is not being a child of a lesbian but dealing with society's attitude. That is what makes the child feel different:

JOHN: 'I worry about the trouble my son might have in the future because of my sexuality, and I do my best to protect him. He is the most important thing in my life.'

ANGELA: 'I have told my eldest child about our family. He is very mature, and I explained to him the difference between privacy and secrecy. I have not told my youngest. He just would not understand ... yet.' Angela's sons are aged thirteen and seven.

PAM: 'I have not told my youngest either. I will "come out" to my ex once I have told my nine-year-old about Jo and me.'

JIM: 'Me and my son discuss the gay issue quite often. At eleven it is tricky to keep it from his friends, but otherwise he seems very okay with it. I even talked to him before my boyfriend moved in. It was important for me to have his opinion, and to make sure he understood what is happening.'

PAT: 'My nine-year-old understands our setup. He has friends to the house and explains the situation to these little boys in a matter of fact way which never seems to need any further explanations.'

Pat said this warmed her heart. She has never seen any young children caught up in taboos. She firmly believes children can accept most things if they are told in a manner they can understand, and 'I know this is true from experience.'

Johnny hoped that by telling his unhappy story about 'coming out' he might help others to avoid a similar painful situation. Johnny had been married for twenty-five years and had two teenage daughters. When he left home, he moved in with a male roommate 'for financial reasons'.

This relationship did not last, and the sadness for Johnny of a failed marriage, a lost lover and an increasingly distant relationship with his daughters meant that he found himself having suicidal thoughts. Johnny believed that his daughters would never accept his homosexual relationships. He decided to try counselling and there he discussed his fears of what could be the worst thing that could happen: that his daughters would reject him. He decided to be open with them, but as he fumbled to find the words his eldest daughter broke in with, 'If it will help, we know why you and Mum split up. We knew your roommate was your lover.'

The girls went on to tell their father that, 'Even Mum is handling it fine now. She's got over her anger about the lies.' His younger daughter, Eve, told her father she would have liked to have talked to him months earlier but didn't know how to bring it up or what to say. The conversation then turned into a long and deep discussion about being gay. Johnny was able to correct many of his daughters' misinformed and stereotyped views about homosexuality. With some embarrassment, Eve could discuss some of her fears and thoughts with her father and sister. Once the air was clear they all felt that they had passed important milestones. A difficult journey had begun for them all. Johnny rather sadly adds a final word: 'Acceptance is not the same as approval.'

> STEPHANIE: *'I have a homophobic daughter of fifty-two. I can't tell you the pain I have felt. She won't allow me to see my granddaughters.'*

> PAULA: *'I was married for seventeen years before taking the plunge. I have two sons of fifteen and eight and they are both fully aware of the situation. I told my elder son almost as soon as I had decided what my future life would be, and he is pretty cool about it all. The little one had it all explained to him over a gradual period in age-appropriate language, since he needed to know if he was going to live with my partner and me. The children chose to live with us but I have always given them the chance to return to their dad if ever they feel the stigma of living with us is too much.'*

As we heard from Ruby and Linda there are lesbian couples where one, or both, have a child from a previous relationship. Frequently we were told that an earlier marriage had happened when there had been no earlier acknowledgement (to self or others) of being a lesbian.

> KRISS: *'I married because it was the thing to do. I liked my then husband, but knew I didn't love him.'*

CATHERINE: *'Our marriage had communication problems from the start. At the time I didn't know why.'*

SALLY: *'We split up. I had not acknowledged or come to terms with the fact I was a lesbian.'*

Sally told us that once she accepted what was going on in her life and who she really was, she met a new partner, Val. As they live in a very conservative area they are not 'exactly out of the closet all the way'. They have decided to be 'out' to families, closest friends and a few workmates. All have been supportive and accepting. Colin, Sally's eleven-year-old son, lives with them. Before Val moved in with Sally, Sally consulted two solicitors about a possible custody battle over the boy with her ex-husband. Their advice was to stay quiet about the relationship until her son was older and if a custody battle came up, Colin would then be old enough to make a choice.

SUE: *'It was better once my father had "come out". Until then I felt a great responsibility because of knowing my dad was gay before my mother did. I had found some books he had hidden. They were all about homosexuality. I accepted it from the start. Once Mum knew, they split up.'*

Sue added that her mother told her brothers and sisters in such a way that they have been totally alienated from their father. This has caused a further split in the family and Sue now aligns herself with her dad and his partner.

SUE: *'I am part of his family. Families are not only about blood – a family is made up of people you love and trust.'*

Sue was adamant that having a gay father has not influenced her sexuality. 'I am heterosexual, but if I weren't it wouldn't bother me.'

Family Occasions

Family occasions are a frequent time of stress. For couples living together, especially if not 'out' to the extended family, these occasions can mean separation at times when, traditionally, families get together.

MARGOT: *'My partner and I and her children became a new family. I was heartbroken, though, when Annie's family invited her and the*

*children for Christmas and I was not included. The worst thing was
Annie and the children went. Our relationship never recovered.'*

From others we heard similar stories, often around events at school:

JIM: *'We all go everywhere together, except school functions. I
agree the world isn't ready for two dads to accompany the boys. I
stay at home. I know I am a parent, but I would never put Liam
and Leo in a position of having to explain me away.'*

JANEY: *'We're not the only lesbian mums at my daughter's school.
My nine-year-old daughter said to me, "There's another girl at
school who has two mums."'*

PATRICIA: *'On Mother's Day both my kids made a card for Jackie.
"To my other mum," it said.'*

BILL: *'No problems, on Mother's Day my boy sends his mother a
card, and on Father's Day I get one. We might have different views
on life, but my ex-wife and I are still parents.'*

Co-parent or Not?

Opinions differ as to the wisdom of the partner becoming a 'co-parent'.
Perhaps the problems which arise are not so different from those faced
by any parent or stepparent, since introducing a new member into a
family always calls for sensitivity and discretion. As with a new
heterosexual partner the children need to be kept informed about the
situation as it develops and a relationship needs to be formed gradually
between the child and the adult.

BARRY: *'No one told me anything. One moment I had a mum and
dad. The next moment Dad left and Molly moved in and just took
over Dad's place, even in the bedroom. I was very unhappy, looking
back I can understand why. At the time I was angry, withdrawn
and very uncooperative according to my school reports. I never
gave Molly a chance, but she did try to be the heavy parent and
encouraged Mum not to be soft on me.'*

To us, it seems that for Barry the issue was not that Molly was a
woman but that his father had, apparently, been replaced and that he
(Barry) was expected to relate to Molly as if she were a parent. We

spoke with Barry at length and he did not, even once, say he had a problem having a gay mum with a partner. What was on his mind was the way he felt they expected him to accept major changes in the adult world, which as a boy of twelve were quite beyond him.

> BARRY: '*I missed my dad – I didn't want another. Ten years on, I am just becoming friends with Molly.*'

Some parents feel anxiety at introducing a new partner of the same sex to their child. Will there be awkward questions? If not from the children, then from other parents? Yet is it anyone else's business? Like any parent introducing a new partner, the decision has to be made about their status and authority in the family. One view is that as with any successful stepparenting, the whole family should take time and care to blend into a new family. Account must be taken of the child's difficulties in having a new parent. The attitude and good will of other adults around will have an influence on this. It is only after sharing tears and joy together that a family can settle into being a family, whether the parents are heterosexual or homosexual. It cannot be rushed; it is necessary to be prepared for a transition period, however good the intentions are.

The primary decision about 'co-parent' status has to be made by the parent, but the views of the child and the new partner must also be considered:

> EVA: '*We really do co-parent. If my daughter calls "Mummy" we both respond.*'

> CRAIG: '*My boyfriend is quite a bit younger than myself. My son's relationship with him is more of an adult friend than another dad.*'

> GEORGE: '*My partner does not even try to act as a parent – it would be inappropriate.*'

> KEVIN: '*My son likes my new partner, but he also likes my partner's ex-boyfriend and I do have a problem with that.*'

> LORNA: '*I would love to have become a mum to my partner's children, but she didn't want this.*'

Lorna highlighted a predicament for many new partners where there is already a child from a previous relationship: what to explain to the children about the significance of a partner, whether live-in or not. Again, this is highlighted if an additional factor is a same-sex partner. Yet this is very similar to what we were told by post-divorce single parents who started dating again, and will depend upon the age of the child.

AMY: *'Children do not see what is to be seen.'*

On the other hand:

CARRIE: *'I thought as they got older they would suspect something and we should tell them about my relationship with their mother, and not let them find out by accident.'*

BONNIE: *'I felt quite elated. I wanted to be seen as a parent to Alice's children. I took them to football practice, I took them shopping and ran them here and there. Yet Alice was not comfortable enough with herself to be sure her kids would not judge her and continue to love her in the same way, if she told them the truth about us. I struggled along with the secret, feeling very lonely.'*

SUSIE: *'My partner was involved with a woman before me. They raised the children and ran the home in the same way as heterosexual couples do. The children saw and heard the fights too. They split up, and I can understand that it would be too difficult for the children to be told yet, that I am their new second mum.'*

This confirms that there are difficult and sensitive areas when introducing a new partner to the children. The pace cannot be forced, and on top of everything else a lesbian or gay partner will have the usual stepparent's anxieties about how to be a second mother or father. Those who did not see themselves replacing the birth parent, seemed to fare best. The same problems arose as with heterosexual families: jealousies, divided loyalties, and no shared earlier history. Often the children were still feeling the effect of the breakup of the family which had nurtured them, so caution and sensitivity were often the keys to success.

GEORGIA: *' I think I am lucky, my daughter likes my new partner. I think I'd have much more trouble if I let a man move in. This way, she thinks I have a friend, and no one is trying to take her dad's place. At least not obviously.'*

JENNY: *'We're okay at the moment. My ex was very violent and the children remember this. They love the calm atmosphere that May and I create. Will they ask questions when they want to know?'*

The age of the children, especially if they are still at school, can affect the way things develop:

BETTY: *'I lived with my partner, Lee, and my two little girls. All was fine until they went to school and began to have friends back to our house. I began to feel uncomfortable and asked Lee to move into the spare room. She was furious and eventually moved to her own flat. We still spend a lot of time together, but there are not awkward questions from the kids now.'*

Children, particularly during adolescence, often have a problem if they feel their parents are different, whether it is because of religion, colour, or the clothes they wear. It is as if they need something to fight against as they develop their own ideas and identity. However, it is psychologically maturing for a child to realize the adult world is made up from different shades of grey, and that this includes sexual orientation.

All Right to Be Different?

So is life for a mother or father 'coming out' any easier now than it was thirty years ago? In some ways yes; in others not at all. Now that militant gays are more in evidence in their fight against discrimination, the public are in fact becoming less sympathetic to the gay cause. This inevitably includes a gay parent who may be struggling to make a major life change. Families where unorthodox sexuality is an additional factor do find themselves under considerable pressure. A single lesbian woman or gay man 'coming out' can today usually find a supportive network, and the loneliness and fear have largely disappeared. Whereas if there is a child from a previous relationship, both men and women are shocked at the venom directed towards them still. Inevitably, this results in it being more usual than not for the truth about a family situation to be covered up. The children in gay families in the United Kingdom are likely to feel isolated, unlike in the United States where, for example, holidays for gay families are widely advertised and family picnics and events are commonplace. A frequent message is that proud parents make proud kids. But this is still whispered in the United Kingdom rather than shouted aloud as it is in America.

We did however hear that Stonewall Parenting Group in London has begun to have children's parties, which are a great success. The group started when a few individuals with parenting problems came together, and with input from professionals began to campaign on behalf of lesbian and gay parenting issues. At the monthly meetings, which are informative and also social, individuals as well as couples can meet to discuss common issues. Couples considering becoming parents can also be part of the group. Stonewall organizes activities for children of all ages while the adults talk. The group is committed to work for a change in the law to ensure that lesbians and gay men have the same parenting rights as heterosexuals. A volunteer who coordinates the group told us, 'we are about to issue a new information pack which will include a list of gay-friendly solicitors who will specialize in custody issues, wills and pension schemes'.

Both parents and children told us that although they felt okay within the family, they did learn to keep it a private matter. They still fear provoking the disapproval which is directed towards gay families if they are open and honest about their lives.

HANNAH: *'I long for the time when people at large will understand that we love our children, and accept it is all right to be different.'*

Doris – now sixty-seven years old, the mother of three children and a grandmother – read an article in a newspaper in the 1960s which changed her life. In a highly exaggerated way it suggested that as many as 25 per cent of married women were lesbian; this helped her to understand herself in a new light. She maintains, however, that as difficult as things were for her then, they are no easier now for the lesbian mother in the United Kingdom.

Babs Greenwood, a grandmother too, spoke with deep feeling when she described the tremendous struggle she had to change her life. Babs has travelled to the United States on several occasions and has been overwhelmed by the opportunities to be found there to be involved with other women. The support, she says, is given freely and is available and accessible. She finds it unbelievable that women today, especially if they are mothers, are still victims of abuse and scorn. Because Babs is not afraid to speak out, women often write to her to ask for help. They tell her, 'I know I am a lesbian. I can't go on pretending. What can I do? Who can I talk to?' She has begun her own telephone helpline, My Mum's Group.

A recent letter to her from a young woman in the Midlands described the way colleagues at work are treating her: 'Your kids should be taken away from you.' Babs was distraught when she thought of the help that would be offered this woman and her children in America. The only help she could give was to put the woman in touch with someone in Australia in a similar situation who is deeply troubled and not able yet to 'come out' herself.

> ALEX: *'I'd love to "come out" as a new family – but my instincts tell me to keep quiet about my private life. I love my kids and I have seen how others can get teased.'*

> CORRINE: *'I "came out" last year. No more living a lie. I thank God every day. My kids are wonderful and so are my grandchildren.'*

Gay families expressed the very same feelings about what is necessary for a successful family that we had heard from heterosexual couples: love, care and respect. In other words, they were saying, it is the quality of parenting which matters above all else, even above the sex of the parents. Strong feelings were expressed endorsing the belief that while children do need parents of both genders in their lives, it may not be possible for them both to be live in the family home.

> *'If we are ourselves our children can get to know us. Certainly if we are acting a part we shall be found out when we get caught without our make up.'* D.W. Winnicott (1969 (1993)) 'The Building Up of Trust' in *Talking to Parents*.

> ALEX, a fifteen-year-old: *'I say to everyone, "What's the big deal? We're just a family. All people are created equal, remember?"'*

And a final message from Brenda Oakes, of Families and Friends of Lesbians and Gays: 'Don't forget "gay" means "good as you".'

6   Grandparents as Parents

> None but the grandparents should ever oversee a child. Mothers are
> only for bearing.
>
> Rudyard Kipling, *Kim*

The Generation Gap

Grandparents have always been looked upon to give support, love and
protection to the children of their own children. Part of the wonder of
being a grandparent is to be a loving, maybe indulgent, figure in their
lives, but at the same time knowing when to retreat into the
background to let the mother and father get on with the actual
parenting. In a close family the arrival of a first grandchild also heralds
the birth of a new generation and the continuity of the line. It is a
comfort for grandparents to see that life does, and will, go on.

Grandparents can be useful for advice, but woe to the grandparent
who believes that children should be brought up in the same way as
they were forty, thirty, or twenty years ago. Grandmas are on hand to
give reassurance – when asked – and to endorse the parenting the
parents feel is right for the child. In this fast-changing world it often
surprises a young mother to find that her parents do know how to burp
a baby, but on the other hand a grandparent can be left in disarray
when, asked to change a nappy, she discovers that unlike twenty years
ago no nappy pins are needed. But on the whole 'Granny's wisdom' is
valued. One grandmother was indignant to find her daughter's baby
presented for minding plus four pages of written instructions.

Often, as can be witnessed on any park bench or any beach, the two
generations find a meeting place of mutual respect and love. Perhaps
the grandparents, relieved of the pressures of bringing up a family, are
more relaxed in offering love and giving way. Comments for us to note
were: 'I'm not in a rush like I was when I was a young mum.' 'I like to
take time to show my granddaughter how to mend things.' 'As a
working grandmother I can afford a few extra treats for my grandchildren, and we often go off on a Saturday to the theatre.' 'I like to tell
them stories about their dad when he was a boy – it passes on a sense
of history.' 'They love to hear how it was for me as a child during the
war.' Observations like this express a sense of cohesion and of the
extended family's intertwined network.

Grandparents can bask in the delights of loving a grandchild; without the stresses of actually bringing up the child, they have the time to enjoy the relationship to the full. And then, as most grandparents are quick to appreciate, the children go home to their parents, leaving the grandparents to get on with their own life. However, the dark shadow of divorce can change all this. How are grandparents to be equipped to deal with the new situation?

PEARL: *'I love my family, It is everything to me. Now two of my children are divorced and I find that difficult to accept. Yet I do what I can and see my grandchildren when I am able. It is easier with my daughter's children because she has custody. But with my son's boy it's harder. They do visit us occasionally, and I keep in touch with him by phone and letter. I believe in the family still, and I feel I am a guardian of the family with my children on one side and elderly parents on the other. Divorce is truly a terrible thing to happen to a family.'*

ANTHEA: *'When my daughter divorced, we had her and the children to stay every weekend. We were a support to them, and we hoped that by creating a secure loving home for two days out of seven for them all, they would and they did become a healthy unit in their own right.'*

Anthea had the wisdom to support her own child's way of parenting, which is especially important when providing backup for a single parent.

Step-grandparents

Becoming a grandparent is a joyful landmark in life: finding yourself a step-grandparent is much more of a hornet's nest. Instead of a newborn baby to adore, it means getting to know children who may already have loving grandparents and who resent the intrusion of new 'grandparents' whom maybe they have not met before, especially at a time when their lives are fraught with new relationships and experiences.

Careful thought needs to go into establishing the bonding of this new relationship and a poor start can take years to overcome. It is as well to be aware that it may not be straightforward to become a step-grandparent. It can often be a question of overkill as we heard from one grandfather:

JACK: *'I was pleased to become a step-grandparent, until I realized that little Paul already had a grandma and grandpa, a granny and granddad and a gran, so where was I to fit in? There are only so many Sunday lunch-times available.'*

RUTH: *'I was thrilled when my son told me he was getting married. I was not so happy when he told me that Susie was divorced and had a thirteen-year-old daughter, Alison. I felt awkward when seeing Alison and never quite knew how to handle the situation. I would not let her call me by my first name as Susie did, but neither would I allow her to call me Grandma.'*

The situation became more difficult when Susie gave birth to a son. Ruth was 'over the moon', but soon the relationships within the family became strained: Ruth was distressed and resentful when her son pointed out that while she brought the little boy toys or sweets, she failed to do the same for Alison.

RUTH: *'Why should I? She's nothing to me, not my blood.'*

Ruth had a kindred spirit in another grandmother, Margery, who also felt she had step-grandchildren pressed on to her:

MARGERY: *'At only forty, I was expected to be a doting granny to my daughter's new husband's children. He was quite a bit older than my daughter, the children were in their teens and were too big for me to cuddle, even if I had wanted to. It was as if the generations had got muddled up. What was I to do?'*

This confusion between the generations is likely to become more common as the number of stepfamilies increases.

LAURA: *'My granddaughter is my stepdaughter's child. I am only thirty-four. A plus is when I mind the baby: my thirteen-year-old can help with the baby-care.'*

AUDREY: *'I tried, but it's hard to be generous in every way to my "steps" as I call them. I have nine grandchildren of my own and I don't need any more.'*

From MILLY, a heart wrenching: *'Lily married my son. She had a little girl already and I loved her dearly. Four years on Lily left Bill, and I haven't seen my lovely step-granddaughter since. It broke my heart. I often wonder how she is and if there is any way I could get back in touch. But Bill says to leave it.'*

Other grandparents identify with Milly's situation and this leads to the fear of wholeheartedly loving a step-grandchild who may disappear at some future date. Blood is thicker than water and although there is no guarantee that contact with grandchildren will last, with step-grandchildren the fear of loss constantly overshadows the relationship.

> KIMMIE: *'I was a step-grandparent while married. Now that we are divorced, my children remain as aunt and uncle to the children, but I have no name. We are in a fog how to explain who I am in words that a three-year- and six-year-old can grasp. Vocabulary does not give us a word for these relationships.'*

> EILEEN: *'My son lived with Erica and her two boys. I had my doubts that it would last and I was right. I know that "second time around" relationships can break down too. I am glad I kept myself to myself and did not get involved with the children.'*

Eileen held back, to prevent possible heartache. This was clear from Rebecca as well:

> REBECCA: *'My son moved in with a girl who has three little kids. I went to visit with good intentions, but when I found out she had the children from three different partners I drew back at once. How could I be sure she would stay with my son? I begged him not to have a child with her. I knew I'd be sad enough if the three went, but it would kill me if a grandchild of my blood was to go too.'*

> BRIDGET: *'No problems, if my son could love his new wife's children then so could I.'*

> JOAN: *'I have six grandchildren, and what a mixture they are. My son has one boy from his marriage and one stepdaughter. My daughter, Becky, decided she wanted a child – no partner, I'm afraid – and had a little girl, Maddie. My other daughter had one child from her first marriage and two from her present relationship. What does it matter? I am "Gran" to all of them. If you want to be a family today, you have to be open-minded about these things. Everything is changing.'*

Joan was pleased to tell us about the pleasure the children brought her. She saw few complications, 'except when trying to explain things to neighbours'. She laughed: 'I can't work out the relationships between them all, and I don't try.' Joan believes the children get along well together on the whole. Joan's daughter, Becky, and Becky's daughter Maddie live with her and there are occasions when Maddie finds it difficult to share when the other children come for weekends to her home.

JOAN: *'Christmas can be a problem. I try to make a family Christmas dinner, but to get them all together can be a nightmare. Becky was angry this year because her daughter Maddie had to have her gifts the Sunday before Christmas to keep in line with the other children who were off to their other parent for Christmas day. It is funny that it is Maddie, of all the children, who often feels left out, and yet it is her home.'*

Parenting your Grandchild

We had not expected to hear so extensively from grandparents who had taken over the role of parents to their grandchildren. Although in some cultures it is usual for grandparents to bring up their grandchildren, this is not so in the United Kingdom. It is completely different from being a grandparent, even a very supportive one, in the background. For if the parents are absent through death or for other reasons, the grandparents become their substitutes, providing nurture, love and every kind of support twenty-four hours a day, seven days a week. We heard from grandparents deeply involved with their grandchildren in a non-traditional way. In the United States 3.7 million children live with grandparents (statistics from Grandparents Information Centre); one third of these children do so without a parent being in contact. Statistics for this country are not available.

The media – when they speak of them at all – speak of 'recycle parents', but on the whole very little notice is given in this country to these surrogate parents who take on (or have thrust upon them) the responsibility of raising another set of children. At a time when most couples are looking forward to relaxing and spending more time with each other they are met by a challenge most rise to meet.

HEATHER: *'My daughter left home when she was fifteen. Ran away, in fact. Three years on I heard from the Social Services: Joanne had died from a drug overdose and she had left a child. What could I do? We took the baby and have had Fiona ever since. I like to feel, now, that we have been given a second chance with a daughter. This time I don't intend to fail and discussion is the name of the game. I suppose we are a new family, and it's no picnic I can assure you.'*

Heather and her husband spoke of the constant pain they felt about Joanne's death. Whilst devoting their time and love to Fiona their heartache is centred around feelings of having failed their only daughter in some way.

> BETTY: *'I brought up my daughter to be loving and kind. I thought I did it right. Now when I see the way she has behaved I have my doubts, doubts about myself. Now I am bringing up Anna I worry how will she turn out.'*

> AGNES: *'My daughter became pregnant when she was sixteen. She went off to live with her boyfriend. She had a baby, Nigel, and moved from one squat to another. What could I do? The worst time for us was when she came home here for a week and, after a midnight telephone call from her boyfriend, said she was leaving again and taking Nigel. It was freezing outside, and I begged her to stay. She went. A month later they were back but not to stay. I asked her to leave Nigel with me and she did. That was four years ago and I have heard nothing from her since. Try explaining that to a five-year-old.'*

> SANDRA: *'My son was seventeen when he got his girlfriend pregnant. We thought she was seventeen too, but she was only fifteen. Her parents said they wouldn't look after the baby when it was born, so I stepped in. I had him from five days old. After a bit she said she would have a go, and I went too so I could teach her Jonathan's routine. She wasn't interested, though, so I left with Jonathan. I have had him ever since.'*

These grandmothers felt they had no alternative but to take on their grandchildren. They had done so willingly and lovingly, but the women were very much aware that they had stepped in at a time in their lives when being a supportive grandmother would have been easier than being once more in the firing line of a hands-on parent.

> VERA: *'My husband and I have been raising our grandson since he was four years old. For the first year I really struggled with having a young child again but I soon came to accept it for many reasons. Most important, we didn't feel that he would have much of a chance with his parents and their lifestyle. His mother, my daughter, never married the father who sees Brian twice a year, and his mum also sees him only a couple of times a year. We have custody of Brian, now eight. My daughter was sixteen when she*

had him and it has been very difficult to be called grandma and grandpa when we look more like his parents. He is a love and I would not change anything at this point in time. It certainly has its drawbacks, but the positive rewards far outweigh the negative. The other point I would like to make is that we are both so much more involved with Brian than we were with our daughters.'

JEANIE: *'My daughter was beaten by her husband and she ended up in a psychiatric hospital. I took little Tracy to live with us, unofficially, almost since she was born, and I got legal custody when she was eighteen months. It has been a bad time, my husband died three years ago from cancer, and I couldn't bring him home to die because of caring for the little one.'*

For a grandparent to become a parent to their child's child – however welcome in some ways this might be – there must have been some tragedy or major disruption for this to come about.

Divorce is not the only trigger: death, desertion, imprisonment and drug abuse play their parts too.

RACHEL: *'When my divorced daughter died from breast cancer there was only me to care for Edgar. I am a widow and felt totally and utterly alone. Having a small boy alienated me from my friends and I knew of no other grandmother in this position.'*

JIM: *'Our daughter decided to have a baby on her own. No father. Okay, fine. Her death last year means we are now parents to a three-year-old grandson.'*

Everyone needs peer support, especially in times of struggle or change:

ANDREA: *'Most of my friends' kids are grown up. The sad part about being a parent again is that my friends have been less than supportive. But I think that for every negative I feel about Clare being with us there is also a plus.'*

MIRIAM: *'My son and his wife separated, and my daughter-in-law kept little Ruth. It got too much for her on her own and the next we heard was that Ruth – three years old – had been abandoned in the street. Social Services got involved, of course, and tried to get Ruth and her mother together again. It didn't work out, and Ruth was placed in a foster home. My son is mentally ill and couldn't have her. My husband and I were heartbroken to know she was not in a*

Jewish home, but we had open access and visited her every week. It took us three years to get custody of her. Her mother does get in touch and we have been told by a child psychologist to let Ruth see her mother, otherwise she may invent a fantasy mother. Ruth asks lots of questions and still gets upset over her mother "leaving her in danger". I cannot forgive my daughter-in-law – despite her being left by her mother when she was a child – and my invalid son couldn't support them.'

We enquired about Miriam's husband. 'Well he's seventy now, and would like a quiet life. But what can you do? We cope.'

SUZANNE: *'The father of my grandsons is unknown. Our daughter put the eldest boy at risk. She asked her dad and me if we would adopt the children to protect them. She visits, sometimes often and sometimes not for months. It is very hard on both boys. She signed the paperwork and we became their legal guardians. When it actually was legal, I didn't think that my feelings for the boys would change. I was wrong. Coming out of court I felt an overwhelming feeling of protection for them. Some might call it the maternal instinct kicking in. I did not expect it. My husband and I are both over fifty years old, not exactly the age for parenting a four- and a six-year-old. We prayed for help and I do sometimes worry about the future of the boys.'*

From Sheffield we heard from Pam. She told us she had so much to talk about, and she did not know where to start.

PAM: *'I care for four of my grandchildren. I have had Candy since she was born. Then my youngest daughter, Doreen, had Paul before she was married. When she did marry, Paul came to live with me. Doreen had three more children, and when the court took them away from her I said I would have two of them. I couldn't take on the new baby too. I already had two at home. The baby is fostered. We had to go through a lot of proceedings with the Social Services – they said they had never seen a setup like mine.'*

A car crash meant the phone rang in the middle of the night for Miles and Eve:

MILES: *'We went to bed grandparents and woke to find ourselves the parents of a twelve-year-old. We all grieved together for the first year, now we are like any family and have our ups and downs.'*

MARIE, a seventy-year-old grandma looking after Alan, aged eleven: *'My daughter killed herself. I love Alan, and every night I pray I will live long enough to see him grown up. I am all he has now. Of course, money is a real problem, but I try to shield Alan from this knowledge.'*

This was only one of many references to financial hardship and of the extra burden on grandparents' shoulders: 'We had our pension and the child benefit', and 'We had saved to travel – thank god we had some money put by.' 'I had no idea children today were so fashion conscious and it costs. As a clergyman's wife I had always relied on the generosity of the parishioners for secondhand clothes.' 'We have run out of money and energy this time around.' Lack of money was a serious problem.

CHRISTINE: *'My grandson was taken away from his mother, who is my daughter, for mental cruelty. We have received no financial help at all, because we couldn't afford to take out a residency order on him. When they finally took Bob's family allowance off my daughter, she denied me access to my granddaughter.'*

PAM: *'Sometimes I have to laugh – a pension book in one hand and a family allowance book in the other!'*

Although it may be hard for their children and grandchildren to believe, the older generation do have a life apart from being a grandparent:

MARY: *'At fifty-five, and a widow, I was at the peak of my career. Then my daughter's divorce and then premature death meant I was a full-time mother again. To be truthful, I am still in shock. I tried to arrange childcare, but the kids had been through so much change that when it didn't work out I gave up my work, so its back into the kitchen for me.'*

BETTY: *'I was an ordinary grandmother working full time, and enjoying having both our daughter's children to stay on a Friday night. Then we discovered Anna was being abused. We went to the hospital, the police and to the Social Services at once. The police were great: they gave us so much support. I had to give up my job, of course.'*

STEPHANIE: *'I am newly married and suddenly had to look after a five-year-old granddaughter from my previous family and it's not easy juggling my roles. Bill, my husband of four years, is angry; his future has been interrupted and our new marriage has not been what he expected.'*

She continued her story by reminding us that 'my divorce keeps giving us problems'. Stephanie and her first husband are still in contact. Her ex-husband would love to be involved with their grandchild but his new wife is not agreeable to that.

STEPHANIE: *'Three years ago I took custody of my grandchild, and this has made such a difference to Bill and me. This is MY grandchild and I know my new husband is having a very difficult time with this. We have special problems in dealing with energy levels, and how to identify with this child. Also how we deal with her anger towards us since she wants to live with her mother, but her mother doesn't want her.'*

Even though it is 'all in the family' nothing must be taken for granted. Consider this warning from one grandparent:

ARTHUR: *'I made sure my grandson became a ward of court – that means that neither of his parents can turn up suddenly and take their child. We are all safer that way.'*

BETTY: *'We have complete protection of our granddaughter. The Social Services agreed we were the best choice. The Child Protection people expected my son-in-law to go to prison for what he did to Anna, but when my daughter stood by him he was just put on probation. But we lost our other granddaughter when we took Anna to live with us. Lee wouldn't come to stay any more. This is just one of the losses my husband and I have had over the last fourteen months.'*

Most arrangements seemed to be less legally binding:

CAROL: *'My son married and they had a baby. I am ashamed to say they didn't take responsibility right from the start. When Belinda was only two weeks old I was having her overnight. They wanted their lives back and continually went to parties. I looked after her a lot. When Belinda was five years old, my daughter-in-law left with another man and they went to Australia. It broke my heart and I had a nervous breakdown. After a year she came back to England as it hadn't worked out.*

They came to me and I took them in and my granddaughter became like another child to me. We tried to have a plan and now my daughter-in-law has Belinda for one week and then my son has her for a weekend, before my week. He doesn't always have her but does when he can – he's young and is trying to build a new life. I worry about her having three different homes and I wish I had more parental rights. It's all so informal but I daren't upset the apple cart or I may end up with nothing.'

ANTHEA: *'Do you count me as a grandparent or as a parent? My husband and I took a young lady in to our home as the result of a crisis pregnancy. She stayed with us until her child was four years old. Naturally our role was that of grandparents and he was taught to see us in that light. When they left us to live on their own, we remained grandparents to Jonathan and we were his babysitters. Then his mother began to get into trouble with the authorities and when he was six the Child Protection people became involved. Eventually, after years of fighting with the authorities, I was granted custody, but my husband was deceased by then. Jonathan does see his mother from time to time but he has lived with me for many years. He is now sixteen and a joy.'*

Second Time Around

'Do you want to talk to us?' enquired Debbie. She went on to explain that she and her husband had taken on the parenting of her sister's children even though, 'We are of an age when most of my friends are grandparents.' And so we unearthed yet another thread of parenting, that of nieces and nephews.

Debbie's sister, Lisa, had been divorced for many years. Her two children, Tom (fourteen) and Alice (thirteen), lived with her and they had no contact with their father. Lisa died suddenly and Debbie and her husband Frank found themselves first-time parents when they were both in their late fifties. Frank found the situation almost unbearable. He grudgingly agreed with his wife that they had no option, but his plans towards a slow and gentle retirement had not included two uncooperative and distressed teenagers.

DEBBIE: *'I have to remind myself daily that Lisa found life heavy going with her children. I don't believe they ever got over their parents' divorce; add on top of that the sudden death of their mother and you can guess the state the children were in. They didn't want to come to us, and they showed their grief for their mother by being as morose and rude to us as they could be. It has not really ever let up but we carry on because to reject them now would really be the end for them.'*

FRANK joined us and continued: *'We didn't know where to turn, you see. We had no preparation. The kids had to move down to Devon and a change of school made things worse. My heart did go out to them in the beginning but it also went out to Debs and me as we tried to rearrange our life.'*

This concerned couple were truly thrown in at the deep end. Adolescence can, in any case, be a turbulent time but Tom and Alice were sullen and resentful and non-cooperative for years.

FRANK: *'It's a strange experience at my age, to be on the mat in front of a headmaster for not controlling a fourteen-year-old who will hardly speak to me.'*

DEBBIE: *'We do our best, but we know it's not good enough. I am physically exhausted most of the time and usually cry myself to sleep at night.'*

FRANK was pessimistic about the future: *'I just don't know, I just don't know.'*

BETTY: *'If it hadn't been for our faith in God we would never have made it this far. We are entirely too old to have these responsibilities thrust upon us again, but these precious children are worth it. None of them asked to be born, and they at least need a chance in this world.'*

PAT: *'Where would the government be if all of these children had to be kept in foster care? For one thing, they wouldn't be able to find that many foster parents, let alone be capable to paying them for what we grandparents do out of love.'*

What was striking was the way that men and women like this rolled up their sleeves and got on with raising a child. Repeatedly they asked us, 'What else could we do?' While many believed they had been given a second chance at parenting almost all spoke of their grief and sense of failure because their children had, as adults, in many cases been unable to accept their responsibility as parents.

Support Networks

To be a parent second time around can be a very heavy burden. In the United States and in Canada support networks for grandparents raising their grandchildren are proliferating. Sylvie de Toledo, a grandmother in California, set out to help others who find themselves struggling to protect their grandchildren. She speaks of the pain:

> SYLVIE: *'You can't make it go away, you can't make it better, but you can hear them and help them to talk.'*

The de Toledo and Brown book *Grandparents as Parents* (1995), has been a source of help for many who find themselves in this situation, by describing how others have managed and by making them aware of the wide network of groups in the United States. The increasing numbers of grandparents in this situation have come together to give them a voice. On the Internet there are forums for grandparents where grandparents worldwide can chat and help answer each other's questions. These are places where grandparents can discuss their worries and share their fears of collapse, and overcome their trepidation about replacing the parents their grandchildren so badly need.

> ROSIE: *'I am a grandparent raising one of my grandchildren. I have had her since her birth. She thinks I am her mum and calls me Mama. Her mother, my child, is referred to by name. Suddenly she is threatening to come home from Ireland and take her back. I can't find any help anywhere. I cried when I found this forum on the Internet.'*

> SANDY : *'I am a granny mum. I am very excited about being able to talk to people who have had to make the same choices my husband and I have had to make. This is the first time I have ever been able to share my feelings and to hear from others who are where I am.'*

> BETTY: *'Help. I am a grandmother whose son has been accused of injuring his child. I am not even considered for custody because I support my son and believe that the incident was an accident. Please help me.'*

In the United Kingdom the Grandparents' Federation offers support. There is one group under their umbrella called the Second Generation Group, near Peterborough. Its aim is to support any grandparent who takes on the arduous task of the second generation parenting role. The group, including two grandfathers who care for their grandchildren full time, meets weekly, and a creche is provided for the under fives. All of these grandparents will tell you that they had no choice but to become the main carers of their grandchildren; but for them the children would have been put into local authority care. Some of the children may at some time return to their parents, particularly if the parents had been young and vulnerable. The organizer of the group, Chris, says they comfort each other and share the anger and sadness that the inevitable upset produces for all concerned. Without exception, at times they all long to be just grandparents again. Each said they couldn't manage without the support of the group. 'We have so many questions to ask, and one of us can usually come up with the answer', was the universal cry. Together they can struggle to find answers to the questions their children ask, talk about their neverending tiredness, and of the grief that has brought the situation about in the first place.

There Is No Other Group Like This One

Noreen Tingle, national secretary of Grandparents Federation, spoke to us of the financial restraints they as an organization are subject to.

> NOREEN: 'We are trying to raise the money to launch other projects. There are many grandparents who would love a support group, but they must be professionally led, and that costs money.'

If a grandparent has a Residence Order – and most do – then a previous Care Order will be put aside and the Social Services have no legal obligation to help the grandparents. Often the grandparents are glad to sever their contact with the Social Services, yet the family problems can be very serious.

> NOREEN: 'Grandparents can find themselves in a very difficult situation – giving up work, and their leisure. Finances can be a very big problem. The Local Authority has discretion under the Children's Act whether to pay maintenance. Without support for the grandparents the child might find himself back in Care.'

> DORIS: 'I had a bad moment or two when my four-year-old granddaughter started school. I thought I would have to leave the group. But no, I can stay as long as I need.'

They told us that grandmothers who do not parent but are 'ordinary grandparents' often ask if they can join, but membership is restricted to those who can share the same worries and fears (and joys) of Second Generation Parenting. Without exception, all in the group felt that they were deprived of being just an ordinary gran – with the opportunity to spoil the children, and then to send them home to mum and dad.

> ANDREA: *'I became an instant grandmother after a crisis phone call. I love my little grandson, but at 3 o'clock in the morning when I am walking the floor I find it difficult to remember this in my heart.'*

Professional advice is more freely on hand in the United States. From the Grandparent Resources Centre in Delaware we heard of Family Circles. Their task is to support grandparents not only with individual needs, but with advice about resources available. From them we heard, 'Being a parent the second time around can be very trying, especially if you had no idea it was coming.'

Statistics from this centre show the main reason for raising a grandchild is because of drug and alcohol abuse. They have asked grandparents to say what the most positive things are about their relationship with the child. The almost unanimous reply was 'love'. When asked to identify the most pressing worry the answer was, first, worry about money, and, secondly, anxiety about care of the child if the grandparents were sick or died.

The Centre is a model example of help for any 'relative caregiver raising others' children'. From this organization we heard that in the last decade the number of children living with grandparents or relatives has increased by 40 per cent. The Centre provides an excellent comprehensive service and their guidebook becomes a bible for anyone in need of advice.

Unhappily, even in America help is not universal, and in the United Kingdom the need for such groups for these second-generation parents will increase and yet so far any support is, as we heard from the Grandparents' Federation, minimal.

> BETTY: *'I read about your research. Apart from the police and social services I haven't talked to anyone about what has happened to our family. If I am honest, I do resent what has happened to us, but we couldn't let her go into Care. I want to read your book, I want to know about other grandparents and the way they manage.'*

JEANIE: 'We live in a small village near Edinburgh. There is no one else caring for their grandchild. Social Services? They did ask, "What can we do?" and then made a pig's ear of it. When I really needed help, they didn't want to know. "You have legal custody now", they said. They made matters worse; they even took me to court for letting my daughter have unsupervised access to my granddaughter. It wasn't true, and the Sheriff was appalled, and said how lucky Tracy was to have me.'

As grandparents and the children struggle to be a family, the considerable saving to society both in financial terms and in the future mental health of the children cannot be estimated. The least we can do is to make sure they are underpinned to ensure these arrangements do not break down.

Revolving Doors

Jenny was the first grandparent we met to use the expression 'revolving door grandmother', and in time the revolving door scenario became familiar to us: it is a sad one, but one which fulfils an important role.

JENNY: 'My daughter Janice can't make a go of relationships. She has had three partners in the last five years. I have rather given up on her, but not on Benny her little boy. When Benny's dad left them, they came back to me and they stayed until Janice met Reg and eventually the three moved away. Nine months later Janice asked me to have Benny whilst she "got on her feet". Okay, I did, but six months later she came and took Benny when she moved in with Charlie. That hasn't lasted, and now Benny is back with me whilst she "sorts herself out". I know what that means, but until she really settles I know Benny will be back and forth.'

UNA: 'My daughter can't make it on her own since her husband left her. She tries, then brings the children to us, then tries again. This causes the children pain, especially the eldest who is nine. What can we do?'

What, indeed? Una, and others, feel that they are in a dilemma; by offering shelter and love to their family, they are torn apart by the upset of it all.

LINDA: '*I was mum to my grandson for six months. My daughter, Susan, left home at sixteen and two years later had a baby. Jeremy's father is a drug addict and has gone to jail. Susan lived with another man, and when he left her Susan began to train as a nurse. At first we paid for a nursery for Jeremy, then he came to us. We had to help. She worked such terrible hours. My grandson was pining for his "dad" and his mum, and was very unhappy. We tailored our life to care for him. But it is the long-term effects which are bad. I lost my grandmother role. Now when he comes to visit he is suspicious and clings to his mother. Before all this he used to love to stay, now he is scared his mum will leave him again. She is in a new relationship, and he is calling her new man Daddy now. It is a parent's nightmare. We have all lost a lot. How will it end?*'

For other grandparents a happier revolving door situation develops:

JUDY: '*After my daughter was divorced, they came to us and we gave our support to her so she could parent her children. We felt by giving a temporary home they would eventually become a strong loving family, which is what happened. It was tempting for us to parent all four of them but we fought those feelings and left the real parenting to our daughter until she was strong enough to make her own home.*'

GRAHAM: '*My daughter-in-law died, and the two boys came to us. Eventually my son decided to marry again. One boy wanted to go to live with his father and his new wife, but not the youngest. I hope he will, in time, but meanwhile he comes and goes. I long for them to have a settled life and we can be grandparents again.*'

Although a revolving door policy does mean an unsettled life for everyone concerned, there is a measure of stability at times for children who otherwise would be lost in the mist of the adults' disorganized life. It is the Jennys and Unas of this world who can put aside their own feelings and reach out to their vulnerable grandchildren. The protection they provide cannot be measured, and it is beyond price.

A Rift in the Family

Some of the grandparents we spoke to had been forbidden contact with their grandchildren, either by one or both parents; perhaps after a family rift, or following a divorce. One of the most painful knock-on effects of divorce can be that children become estranged from one half of their family. The long shadow of divorce cruelly affects Hilary's life:

> HILARY: *'I kept telephoning my ex-daughter-in-law and inviting her and the children to stay for the weekend. But she didn't like the idea of staying in the house where her ex's new wife stays, so refused. I miss out and so do the children.'*

A disagreement about a lifestyle brought about the crisis in Laura's family.

> LAURA: *'My son and daughter-in-law have two lovely girls. I couldn't stand back and not comment on the way those youngsters were neglected. They were left on their own at nights and I know my son is into drugs. I had to speak up, and finally I was told I would never see any of them again. And I haven't. Do you think my granddaughters will think I just disappeared? Will it harm them? Is there anything I can do?'*

Laura is haunted day and night by anxiety about her granddaughters. Any mail sent is returned unopened and she is tormented by the thought that the girls will believe she abandoned them. Laura and John feel the loss of their family constantly. Time is not helping, and the pain grows daily. Laura has left a letter with her solicitor to be forwarded to her granddaughters after her death. In it she explains her side of the story and tells them of her abiding love of them.

Rona Coutts is very involved with the Grandparent Support Organisation (GSO).

> RONA: *'When my daughter and I quarrelled she told me I would never see my grandchild again. It took me over three years to obtain a contact order via the court. Sadly, my daughter didn't comply with the order and there was nothing I could do. Apparently, the courts don't like to enforce these types of orders as it is said it might put undue stress on the child. I have since learned that the Children Act states that grandparents do not have preferential treatment and are treated as any other third party. I have not seen or heard from my granddaughter in over six years.'*

A grandmother who had been denied contact to her grandchild initially formed a support group, which consisted of six grandparents. From this the GSO developed into what it is today with a support system throughout England and Wales. The organization works in connection with a team of legal experts, and also offers its members support, both emotional and practical. They are there to provide help to grandparents who have problems in maintaining contact with their grandchildren. In their information booklet they emphasize their message that it is important that a child knows his or her family history and heritage, 'It gives the children a sense of stability and belonging to be aware of their roots.'

There is very little a grandparent can expect as 'of right' in the United Kingdom. The parents of the very many divorced and estranged couples often find themselves cut off from contact with them and their children. And if a couple have remained partners and not been married the grandparents have no legal right to see their grandchildren. The fact that a child then loses one whole side of his or her family is not taken into consideration, and yet the damage that is done to the child because of this is enormous. No one should forget that a half of a child's genes comes from one set of grandparents.

The Grandparents' Federation is also inundated with requests from sad and anxious grandparents who ask for advice and support over their lack of contact with their grandchildren. Grandparents seek advice if they want to look after a grandchild in Care on a long-term basis. The Grandparents' Federation can help by providing a professional person to work with a grandparent in some cases. Where a family feud in the wake of a divorce or separation has caused a breakdown in communication, they offer a willing ear and practical suggestions. There is continued sadness and stress in the lives of so many grandparents who are grieving for their lost grandchildren. Illness and depression are rife among sufferers from the fallout of a family collapse. Often the grandparents are the unconsidered part of the misery of divorce. Many spoke to us of their heartache, for it is difficult for them to find help.

One grandmother, May, has begun her own informal telephone helpline to talk to bereft grandparents. She is shocked by the number who contact her and who ask such questions as, 'Should I drive past my grandson's school in the hope of seeing him?' She told us of one unfortunate grandparent whose son worked abroad and so she became surrogate mother, having sole charge of the girls during their father's absence. She then received a letter from her ex-daughter-in-law to say that after the remarriage she wanted her daughters back. This woman has not seen her grandchildren since.

Gail spent many hours talking to us of her agony of losing a ten-year-old granddaughter, because of her son's divorce.

GAIL: *'That was it. I have begged my daughter-in-law to let me see Iris but she won't. She used to say she would, but then didn't turn up. My son has moved to the other end of the country, so he doesn't help.'*

Gail, like so many other grandparents, felt utterly helpless.

> GAIL: *'What should I do? I did phone the other day and my sweet granddaughter answered the phone. I said, "It's Granny," and suddenly the phone was taken away from her and the receiver put down. Would this have hurt and confused my granddaughter? Am I the only grandma like this?'*

As our research shows, she is not. In some ways this comforted Gail, but also spurred her on to write a letter to her local paper. It was printed under the heading 'We have feelings too' and described the situation for many grandparents who are unable to see their grandchildren. She has had a certain amount of feedback and hopes to start a local support group for other bereaved grandparents.

> GAIL: *'Yes, that is what we are, bereaved.'*

May, who started Grandparents and Parents Support (GAPS), summed up: 'I understand from experience and try to give them the strength to accept since there is nothing I can do to change the situation, although really that is what they want.' She believes that few people appreciate the ongoing emotional pain caused by the loss of children and grandchildren by separation. According to May, when a grandparent longs to nurture a grandchild and contact is denied, the feeling is of total impotence.

> GARY: *'My son and his wife divorced, it was very acrimonious. The outcome was that he doesn't see his children and that suddenly meant we were no longer able to see them. You can't imagine the pain for us.'*

> LESLEY, his wife, continued: *'It happened so suddenly. One Christmas a loving family time, the next Christmas a divorce and my daughter-in-law had gone to New Zealand with the children. My son has his own problems, but for me it's a tragedy. Why did she have to divorce me too?'*

Questions and Answers

All grandparents standing in as parents felt they should answer the questions put to them by the children of their children in a positive manner. Questions from the children about why they lived with their grandparents, why they didn't live with their own parents, and why their grandparents looked different from their friends' parents, came in various forms, but they always came. It is important to answer questions as and when they arise on any subject, but not necessary to give more information than the child is really asking for, whether it is about sex or an aspect of family relationships.

MARY: *'When the time comes, I shall answer his questions truthfully without being "painfully" honest.'*

PAT: *'My grandson is only seventeen months old. I wonder what I'll say when he realizes that all children don't live with their grandparents, and why does he?'*

JOAN: *'Oh the whys! I try to give edited answers and I think the important thing is to make sure we all spend a lot of time remembering the fun things that they did with their parents before they died and not to dwell on only the bad things.'*

After a split in the family some grandparents take sides and add to the tension of a divorce. To do this by speaking ill of one or both parents or in-laws in front of the grandchildren can only distress them and eventually may distance the grandchildren by adding to their confusion.

At times every child feels he is different from his friends – and this can cause anxieties, especially in a family situation when children are cared for by someone other than their parents. When a grandparent is caring for a grandchild, the generation gap can show. This can be in a physical way too as the grandparents who are parents 'second time around' were quick to tell us.

FREDA: *'We loved caring for our baby grandson. It was only when he began to be quick on his feet in the park I began to feel my age. I couldn't catch him.'*

Freda's husband, John, agreed and said:

JOHN: *'I try to play cricket and football as I know their dad would have done, but I just can't keep it up. They get quite rattled when I say I have to rest.'*

PAM: *'I might have less energy, but I have much more patience.'*

ANDREW: *'I play the father's role up to the hilt, but then Sports*

Day comes around and I know Bob doesn't want me to try the fathers' race.'

Andrew remembered the occasion when he put himself forward, only to find his name scratched by his grandson. They didn't speak about this to each other, but it was clear they both had their own pain about this event.

Often a fine line has to be drawn between appeasing a child's curiosity, and hurting his feelings and self-esteem – especially when there are questions about why parents are not there to care for a child.

BETTY: *'My daughter-in-law had fourteen affairs during five years of marriage. Our son was stupid enough to take her back each time. She has been into heavy drugs since she was fourteen – we found this out later. The biggest question and the hardest to answer is why does Mummy like men better than us? They have seen her go through one man after another depending on who can supply her the easiest. Our standard answer to that is that your mother still loves you but she has a sickness and until that is cured she is unable to take care of you and be your mummy. They just cannot be told that her drugs are more important to her than they are.'*

GEORGE: *'Our grandchildren, seven and nine, eventually came to live with us. They had seen their father beat up their mother many times. They knew their parents were now both in prison – drugs, I'm afraid. It brought tears to my eyes when the eldest asked, "Why don't you and grandma ever fight?" I tried to explain that adults don't have to spend their time fighting; we can disagree without that.'*

ALICE: *'My granddaughter asks constantly, "Why does God let people do bad things and leave their children?" Try explaining to a six-year-old that God gave us free choice and sometimes we abuse that gift. Their eight-year-old cousin finally took care of that by telling them that, "Satan used to be an angel but he was bad and God threw him out of heaven. Now some people love Satan more than God." Very simplified but very effective.'*

Society now has a wide variety of family constellations and it is almost certain that a child will not be the only one in his school class who does not live with both parents in the old 'conventional' family. Less than a quarter of British households are now traditional families, made up of a married couple with dependent children, and this is reflected in every classroom. Hopefully, professionals – such as teachers and doctors – are now more sensitive to variants in the family structure; they should be available to answer and give guidelines. But at a time of change in the family structure, children may turn first to their grandparents for answers and it is important that the answers are presented without bias.

JUDY: *'I would never say anything derogatory about either of Jason's parents when he asks me about them.'*

MATILDA: *'My grandson asked me, "Do I come from a broken home?" I said, "Certainly not. Grandpa and I have mended it."'*

MICHELLE: *'I refer my grandson to his parents to answer his questions.'*

Some questions were asked over and over again: 'Why aren't my parents together?' 'Why don't I live with Mum and Dad?' 'Why did they have me if they don't want a life together?' 'Who do I look like?' 'I don't want another dad, why is Mum getting married again?' 'I don't like my stepmum, can I live with you?' Some typical comments from children are hurtful: 'How can you understand. Things are different nowadays.' And the age-old 'You don't understand' from an adolescent can have a specially hurtful ring about it to grandparents. So, too, can 'My mum or dad wouldn't make me.'

LILY: *'It would be so easy to tell them that one of the reasons they live with us is because we care enough to set down rules and expect them to be followed. There have been times I have felt like telling them their parents are self-centred brats who need to grow up. My husband and I made a pact we would never do this.'*

When Belinda was asked by her grandson if he could come and live with her after his father had remarried, she replied: 'I told my grandson his dad is trying to build a new family for him and he should help by giving his stepmother a chance.' Questions after questions were asked by the children and it did seem an additional burden on grandparents struggling to be good parents. A common refrain was 'the hardest thing is to keep our mouths shut about all the things their mother/father has been and is doing'.

POLLY: *'I have had Bobby since he was nine months old, and so am able to answer many of his questions about when he was a baby.'*

JENNY: *'I always reply to Olwyn that he is right to ask these questions and I reassure him it's okay to ask. The answers aren't so easy to find. He asks, "Why didn't they get married?" "Did they fight a lot?" "Why am I living with you and not my mum and dad?" and "Why did they have me if they don't live together?"*

FIONA: *'I tell my granddaughter we love her, and so do her parents but the problem is neither of her parents can really take care of her.'*

MARSHA: *'I say to Billy, that his parents didn't realize when they had him how hard it is to look after a child, but they do love him in their own way and felt it would be best for him to be with us.'*

MIKE (aged sixty-one): *'It breaks my heart that Stanley keeps asking me what will happen to him when I die.'*

PAM: *'I have to live long enough to bring these children up. Last week I had angina diagnosed by the doctor. Oh well, at least I know now I have a heart.'*

After talking to Pam at length about the care of her four grandchildren, there is no doubt that she has a heart.

ANNA: *'My grandchildren were sexually abused by their father. God knows how I will deal with their questions, but I know I shall have to one day.'*

BILL, a worried grandfather: *'There are so few guidelines concerning grandparents raising grandchildren. For a long time I thought Val and I were the only ones of our generation bringing up our children's children.'*

GILES: *'My grandson looks upon us as his parents; he knows no other. I know when the lad is older we will have to go into more detail. The only question he has asked so far I couldn't answer was, "Why do you take so many pills, other dads don't?"'*

In contrast other grandparents told us a big plus in second-time parenting was having many younger friends, parents of their grand-children's friends. Joining the PTA keeps them young at heart.

CORINNE: *'I know all the latest pop songs, and I know what to value in a child. With my son I was always cleaning and cooking.*

Now if Cory wants a game of Monopoly or to go to the park, I think, so what if supper is late, and I play. But on the other side of the coin, Mark and I feel cheated out of enjoying our later years together. I love being with the kids but there is never a break ... I've done this before.'

SALLY: *'My granddaughter and I talk and talk. I never did that with my daughter.'*

MURIEL: *'I don't feel I am in my sixties. I suppose my story is unusual. I am a widow, and after my daughter died my son-in-law moved in with my little granddaughter to live with me. Six months later he asked me to marry him and after a lot of soul searching I did. We have made a happy family again. Only at times I feel bad that I have everything that should have been my daughter's. Still I know she would have been happy for us. She did not have a jealous bone in her body.'*

ALISON: *'We care for our eight-year-old grandson. Oh, it is very hard sometimes. Yet only yesterday I was looking through his RI book and read the following,"I trust my Grandpa because he is honest, always there for me, and helps me with my problems." When I think of what that child has been through, reading that brought tears to my eyes.'*

SIMON (her husband): *'I am concerned about when he reaches an age when he will feel that life would be more fun if he were living with mum and dad.'*

This is frequently a problem when children of divorce lose contact with one or both parents. Of course, if they do see one or other of the parents, children are not above a little gentle blackmail when the going gets tough: 'My dad wouldn't say that' or 'My mum would have let me ...' are strategies that should not be encouraged. A line should be drawn and the position made clear.

One particular area of doubt is pinpointed in the question posed by Gladys:

GLADYS: *'Should I let my grandson call me Mum?'*

There is no set answer. Some grandparents told us that if the child's mother was truly absent they did slip into being called Mum. Others found alternatives, as we heard from 'Grannymum'. Others were adamant that a child should be aware of the different status of the relationship.The child may well have a view of his own about this. Jack, aged seven, had his own word 'Gram' which satisfied him as an amalgam of gran and mum.

PAM: *'Two call me Nana and two call me Mum. It doesn't matter really. They all know I am their mum.'*

MURIEL: *'My granddaughter still calls me Gran. It often makes people puzzled about our family.'*

JEANIE: *'My Tracy calls me GrannyJeanie. It was her idea.'*

What if a child is teased at school about having old parents? Pam did not think this had ever been a problem for her grandchildren.

PAM: *'They are not the only ones. Emily lives down the road and I heard her say, "I'm lucky, I have got two mums and two dads, but my real mum is my granny." Kids adapt.'*

It is important to make the school aware of the family situation, especially if it changes. And the child should be reassured time and time again that he (or she) is loved and it doesn't matter that his 'parents' are his grandparents; it is nobody else's business.

Victims of Circumstance

We were overwhelmed with information from grandparents, from middle age to old age, whose lives were being affected by family crisis. Whether a step-grandparent or someone parenting for the second time, or a person grieving for a 'lost grandchild', all these people had one thing in common: they were victims of circumstance. While some braced themselves to take on parental duties, others mourned the loss of their status as grandparents. When we wrote *Where's Daddy?* (1996), we were made aware of the extreme importance of grandparents for children, especially for children of divorced or separated parents. For those single parents without an extended family we urged them to 'find grandparents wherever you can – look around the neighbourhood and borrow other people's – look for a grandmother when looking for a babysitter – but find them.' The Grandparents' Federation has monitored a scheme for three years which brings together youngsters who do not have a 'supergran' or 'gramps' with other people who can act as grandparents. They hope to extend this scheme when finance is available.

ELLIE: *'When things were very bleak indeed, I reminded myself that grandchildren are our hope for the future. So I found it in myself to give hope for the future to my grandchildren.'*

PAM: *'Sometimes I ask myself why can't my daughters care for their children. Is it my fault? I don't think so, but why?'*

However hard it is to parent again, we should keep in mind the agony of those *not* in contact.

JENNY: *'I would love to be a mum a second time around. My youngest daughter started taking drugs at school and then three years ago just disappeared. Recently, I managed to find her and she had a baby two weeks old. I visited her and asked to see the baby. Both my daughter and her partner were drunk, and I was in despair at the sight of the baby. They told me to leave. I have alerted the Child Protection people. I can't save my daughter, but I will do my best for my grandchild.'*

Perhaps Christine speaks on behalf of all the children brought up by grandparents:

CHRISTINE: *'My two sisters and I were brought up by our grandparents from the ages of twelve, ten and five. I am the youngest. I can't tell you enough how much we appreciated our grandparents' devotion. They both worked long after retirement age, and both said they would be happy as long as they lived until the three of us were independent. They both died last year, within two weeks of each other. We were, indeed, raised by truly GRAND-parents.'*

And from JACKIE (aged fourteen): *'I don't know where I'd be without Granny – but I do cry sometimes and wish I was with Mum and Dad. I haven't seen them since I was six. Do you think they still love me, and remember me?'*

7   Double Families

Marriage is now a high-risk enterprise

Lawrence Stone, *The Family, Sex and Marriage*

Keeping the Balance

We have already seen in Chapter 4 how being part of more than one family can be fraught with difficulties; how time spent with children from a previous relationship can cause resentment and jealousy for the subsequent partner and children.

> BRIAN: *'You can't be in two places – and I know both my wife and ex-wife suffered from feeling neglected whilst I tried to be a good father, a stepfather and then a dad to a new baby.'*

But how much more difficult is it when one parent is an integral part of more than one family? Indeed, when *one* parent has *two* families? In a 'double' family situation, unlike the normal stepfamily, the main person shares his or her time equally between the two families. In the United Kingdom it is, of course, illegal to be married to two people simultaneously. But being the head of two families concurrently and sharing time between them, as if the other did not exist, is not against the law. Nor is it illegal to have children with different partners at the same time. More often than not, the existence of a second family is kept a secret, even from the lawful wife. And without the openness of everyone knowing the situation the disclosure can trigger a great deal of pain. For this reason it was not easy to find people in this situation willing to talk to us about their way of life. It is easier to discuss when both 'wives' have known all along about the other family.

In this chapter we are not considering the man who has brief relationships, fathering two, three or maybe more children. We are looking at family situations where there are indeed two families coexisting with or without the knowledge of the other. And in this age of equal opportunities we still did not find a single example of the woman being the linchpin of two families simultaneously.

Fred, the father in two families where both women know of the situation, is blissfully sanguine about it. He told us that as the children grow up they will realize that their father, like so many of their friends' dads, is very busy, often away and can't always be where he's needed!

EMILY (Fred's wife): *'We're not thrilled about it and sometimes there's trouble but we all put up with the situation because we haven't found a better arrangement.'*

Emily told us that the children of her family (aged two years and four months) have no idea of their parents' unconventional setup, because they would be too young to appreciate its meaning. However, this situation will be difficult to maintain in the long term since both of the father's families live in the same small town on the south coast.

Financial security is a factor in this kind of situation. Fred could not afford two families without the legacy he inherited.

FRED: *'I suppose how we live just came about. It never came to the point of choice, so we have carried on, with everyone pleased with the way things are for them. I don't regret it, although I wouldn't go about advising this kind of family life for others.'*

Not surprisingly Fred later told us that sometimes he gets tired, very tired, and dreams about having a relationship with a woman with no children. Meanwhile he considered himself 'married' to both women and committed to family life in two homes. But it is not conceivable that Fred's situation can go on indefinitely in the simple direct way he described. There are seven people involved in this constellation. On the surface Fred is coping and Emily is complacent, but what about the mother in Fred's other family?

LAURA, the mother of Fred's second family: *'It is quite incredible what you can block out if you want to. Fred is such an amazingly strong character. He makes it all seem fair and right. I feel that the pain of losing him is not worth the confrontation and inevitable fracas.'*

She went on to add that living a lie is a big strain and that her parents, both in their eighties, have no idea about the real situation; they think Fred travels a lot, and that Laura is prepared to put up with it. Moreover, Fred's teenage sons by Laura are completely unaware of their father's complicated arrangements. In his darker moments Fred contemplates the possibility of them questioning his frequent absences, especially at holiday time.

Mandy shows us another aspect, where the woman has an interest in keeping the situation as it is.

MANDY: *'I know he lives with someone else a few days each month. He tells me he's on business. But I don't want to lose him. If I tell him I've found out, then it will force him into choosing between us and then he may leave me and our little boy. I couldn't bear that, so my silence is my protection.'*

CARLA: *'I have a five-year-old daughter with Jim. He and I live together for one weekend a month and three nights a week. Last year his wife found out, which was okay but what I dreaded was Jim leaving her. I really love Jim but I know that I couldn't cope with living with him full time.'*

We asked about Carla's daughter and whether she was affected by her father's frequent absences. Is she curious?

JIM: *'We often talk about what and when we will tell her that I have another family, but until something changes, what is the point? Anyway I don't think she would find it odd until she is old enough to realize I am a "husband" to both women. After all lots of her mates' mums or dads have "other families", and for a five-year-old the details are not important, are they?'*

CARLA: *'Jim and I often argue about it. I was all for getting everyone together and bringing it all out in the open, and talking the situation over. But we've been advised that his other children, all in their teens, will be devastated. The pain and confusion they will find themselves in the middle of, would possibly destroy them and their family ideals and their future chances of making stable relationships for themselves. What children want is a daddy like other children's daddies.'*

Erica told us that she was a happy mother and wife, despite knowing about her husband's other family. When her husband died suddenly from a heart attack, before any of the children knew anything about the other family's existence, the two women met shortly afterwards and talked. But they decided never to speak or see each other again. 'What is the point?' queried Erica.

SHEILA: *'I know about his other family; he thinks I don't. To give him credit he does go out of his way to be discreet. Is this good or bad? Why would I want to mention it? I am happy with my life. If things changed or perhaps if I met someone else that I wanted to spend time with, only then might I want to talk about it.'*

JO: *'I got suspicious of Patrick. He came home late all the time and smelt of perfume; there were odd phone conversations too. One day I got so furious that I called him at work and accused him of having an affair. He said I had put two and two together and got five. He denied that anything was going on and got very angry with me. I did what many, many wives do I'm sure, I convinced myself that it was all in my imagination. More and more signs surfaced and it became impossible for me to ignore. When I spoke to Patrick about it again, he said that if I didn't stop nagging on about it, I would drive him into the arms of another woman. I thought I would wait for it to end. But we are now four years down the line and I am finding it hard living with a man I share emotionally and physically. Last Christmas I had to confront him and he broke down and told me the truth. He said he would leave Pam like a shot, but they now had a nine-month-old daughter and he felt tied to them too. I wished I hadn't asked. I can't imagine starting again, so I grin and bear it.'*

Double lives can often continue in this way because of the fear of losing something or someone. The very fear of the unknown or of changes likely to happen makes this unsatisfactory *status quo* an acceptable way of life: better the devil you know – literally. So, the implicit or explicit agreement of all parties *for their own reasons* must be seen as playing a large part in these charades. Lips are sealed and tongues bitten in order to maintain a front.

Agnes believed that double families come about by accident. She couldn't imagine anyone planning to have two families:

AGNES: *'I fit into several categories. My relationship with Arthur began with an affair. I knew he was married. He did leave his wife and came to live with me and I got pregnant. That was planned. What wasn't planned was that his wife said she would take him back, and he went. Where did that leave my daughter and me? We all got together and the outcome was that although he went back to Carol we were still his family too. To be fair, we are not neglected and he spends as much time with us as he can. We even have him on alternate Christmases. My little girl is six now and when Arthur goes away, I tell her he is going to see another mummy and her little boy. Because I'm okay about it, I think she is too.'*

Yet planning did seem to be a factor in Joan's husband's life.

JOAN: 'I had no suspicions at all. Then Bob said he was going to leave me and the kids. He was going to his "wife" and two children in Geneva. "It is not an affair," he said over and over again, "they are my family." He began to hint that he could still "visit" us, and the children need not be told. "Don't even think about it", I said. I have been alone now for three years. I am not so sure I was right. I am very lonely, and the children really miss their dad.'

Annie heard about our research into families and offered to tell us about her circumstances: they had been ongoing for seventeen years, and first she wanted our assurance that we would respect her beliefs and not challenge her way of life.

ANNIE: 'We do not have a hole in the wall situation, and I need to make that clear. When I first met and fell in love with Alex at work I knew he was married. It just happened that his wife and family moved to live in the country and he needed somewhere to stay in town. Of course he came to me during the week and our life together began. I knew from the start he would return home to Dorset every Friday, Saturday and Sunday, but I also knew he would be with me all the week. Barbara would telephone him here during the week, and so would the children. I have no doubt at all they knew about our life together. We just never discussed it. Friends knew if they wanted to see us it had to be during the week. It is now I have a worry looming: what happens when we retire?'

Getting older introduces all kinds of problems into family life and, as Annie was acknowledging for the first time, two families sharing one man have a particular agenda of difficulties.

BETTY: 'Oh! Don't do it. Don't be part of a deception. I "agreed" and Bob lived with both families all the time the children were growing up. And NOW he has made a choice, and he hasn't chosen me. I am old, bitter and alone.'

In the Background

Florence met with us to 'set the record straight'. Not all 'other women' were as wicked as they were painted. Florence, a civil servant, said that she had always been shy and had lived with her parents until they died.

Then at the age of forty-eight she began to care deeply for a colleague whom she knew was married. Gordon invited her to go on holiday and while they were in the Lake District he put a proposal to her. He told Florence he loved her deeply, but would never, could never, think of divorcing his wife Greta, or harming his two children by causing a split in the family. His suggestion was this: he would spend three nights a week and some weekends with her, share expenses, share a life, take holidays together, but he would never be able to marry her. This Florence agreed to, and thus began a double life for Gordon which ended only with his death twenty years later. Florence wanted us to know this was not an affair, but a life spent together, though she knew how deeply he cared for his sons from his other family. His absence from them was explained by 'work commitments' and his hobby of mountain climbing. Florence said it was surprisingly easy to get into this way of life, and many friends in London saw them as a devoted couple.

FLORENCE: *'Of course he spoke about the children. I knew when he became a grandfather. I knew his wife had green fingers and liked to sew. She also ironed better than I did, so most of his shirts went home. It didn't really matter. I had a great deal. We had the most wonderful holidays, I never pressed for more.'*

Florence was adamant that there was no heartache, even at times when she was alone.

FLORENCE: *'I knew he would have loved to be with me only, but it was not to be. He was an honourable man.'*

At his last Christmas, Gordon – who had always been generous – gave Florence a large amount of money 'for the future'. In the New Year he told her of an illness, recently diagnosed, which would soon prevent him from being away from home. In February they said their goodbyes and in April Florence read of his death in *The Times*.

FLORENCE: *'I didn't go to the funeral. It wouldn't have been right. I had found my own way to say goodbye. I wonder if his wife ever knew about me? I never asked.'*

When telling us about his own stepfamily Gerard mentioned how his aunt had been part of a complicated family situation. Only after her death had Gerard been told of the 'arrangement' his Aunt Polly had had for years. Gerard remembers his aunt leading an exemplary life and as a widow being a respected member of the family. However, her 'husband', who 'travelled' a great deal, had in fact been married to a woman in Wales. Polly knew this, but it was a secret to the rest of the family. One winter he failed to come home and eventually Polly and her sister gathered some clues and went to a village. Discreet enquiries led them to a house Polly had heard described in detail. One look at the visible mourning in progress made clear what had happened, and they left without making their presence known. It was never referred to again within the family.

Surprise After Death

Amazingly, the discovery of a second family can come as a complete surprise after the death of a father. This happened in a very public way after President Mitterrand's death in France. Although in 1994 *Paris-Match* had made some disclosures, it was only when the former President's illegitimate daughter stood beside her half-brothers at the funeral, that his daughter's existence was publicly acknowledged and recognized. In accordance with her father's dying wishes Mazarine, aged twenty-one, took her place at his funeral for the world to see. Anne, Mazarine's mother and Mitterrand's longtime mistress, walked just a few paces behind his dignified widow, Danielle.

Mitterrand's two 'widows' and children grouped around his coffin made an unusual sight. In public it was a final acceptance, but who can estimate the amount of grief in private? Mme Mitterrand – the mother of his sons – had never agreed to recognize the position of her husband's mistress and of their daughter during her husband's life. Yet, it was not an affair with Anne. He had been very involved with his second family, travelling abroad with them for holidays, and dividing his time between his two lives and two homes. When quizzed by journalists about his hidden family shortly before his death, he shrugged off the questions with, 'So what?' He must have known what the impact would be if he had been open about this relationship during his lifetime. Only after his death could both families be on view for all the world to see. We can assume the families left behind are only now beginning to sort out the legacy of a father's tangled relationships.

In a less public way the same situation affected Mark:

MARK: *'It wasn't until my dad died that we had any idea at all that he lived with and presumably loved another set of kids and a wife.'*

It was when going through his father's papers after his death that Mark began to read items in bank statements that made no sense at the time. As Mark slowly gathered evidence of his father's secret life, he felt a dilemma facing him: whom should he tell? His sister, his mother? Mark believed he was in a similar position to the one his father had found himself in and the urge to continue the cover-up was strong.

Eventually Mark decided to visit his father's other family. The door was opened by a pleasant-looking woman, surprisingly like his own mother in appearance. He was startled to be greeted with the words, 'Are you Mark? Come in, I have waited for you to come.' It took many visits and hours of talking before Mark felt he could fully understand the circumstances.

MARK: *'It helped that I felt comfortable with my .... what do I call her? .... she began to feel like a stepmother. I liked her.'*

Mark still found it incredible that his father had left his affairs in such a way that posthumous discovery was inevitable. He had made provisions for both families after his death but Mark found it hard to forgive his father for giving him no warning of what was to come.

Mark's rapport with his stepmother made it more difficult since he began to have some sympathy for his dad. But one look at his grieving mother reinforced his growing belief that he should not tell her about his discovery. Mark's increasing discomfort at meeting with Sally and her sons meant he felt estranged from his own family. He met his half-brothers and liked them too. Yet he could not come to terms with comprehending how and why his father had let this happen. Mark searched his memory for his father's frequent absences and felt fury at remembering times his father was needed at home, but was busy elsewhere. It was at Sunday lunch with Sally that Mark knew he had to make a choice. He felt he was caught between two lives and could not continue in this way without going under. He was distressed, too, that he had to lie to his mother about his whereabouts.

MARK: *'I told Sally of my decision that I would not visit again. My father had made a terrible mess and I could not clear it up.'*

This happened nine years ago, but Mark still does not feel free of it all. He is haunted with the sadness of missing his father now, just as at times when he was growing up. He is saddened when his mother still talks of what an upright hard-working man his father was.

MARK: *'I realize I didn't know my father at all. Until now I have told nobody about my discovery. I have never married.'*

In his autobiography, *Luckier than Most* (1990), the actor David Tomlinson reveals that his father led a double life. As a child David sensed a strange air of mystery and tension in the home. He was, however, in his forties before he discovered the reason. His father had four children by David's mother, with whom he lived from Friday to Monday, and seven by another woman whose home in London he shared during the week. The division of time was strictly kept to, and for David and his brothers there was an absent father during the week.

The deception was uncovered by Tomlinson's brother, Peter, when he was middle-aged. Until then they had believed their father lived at his club in London during the week. His brother's initial discovery led Tomlinson to uncover the full truth. Although for some years they had had a suspicion that their father was 'up to something', they had no idea how large that 'something' was.

Now in his eighties, Tomlinson reflects on his father and his father's extraordinary life. He described his father to us as, not surprisingly, always preoccupied, and a man who found it difficult to relax. In old age, after the death of both women, his father would talk to David about the complex situation, which had not been without strain. David had in fact, by chance, seen his father's 'other' wife on two occasions. Both times he was struck by the likeness to his own mother, both in appearance and dress. His mother had been kept totally in the dark, and although Clarence Tomlinson was a fairly wealthy man, she was kept short of money and 'not allowed' to leave Folkestone to visit London. It would have been too risky. It seems that Clarence Tomlinson had two loyal secretaries who helped him keep his life in order. After his father's death, David asked them if they knew of any other women. They replied, 'Oh, only the casual ones.' According to David, his father never made a mistake with names or details, and always had a 'plan of campaign'. Later David was to understand why this organization was so important. David Tomlinson had the following conversation with his father just before he died at the age of ninety-six.

CLARENCE TOMLINSON: *'If I had my time all over again, I'd do it all over again.'*

DAVID: *'Oh, you wouldn't.'*

CLARENCE TOMLINSON: *'Oh, yes I would!'*

All's Ill That Ends Ill

Is it ever possible to love and care for two families and to juggle the responsibilities of both? To continue to be a father to a child of a broken marriage is so difficult that 50 per cent of men do not continue to see their children six months after separation (a statistic from Families Need Fathers). So how much more difficult must it be to keep two families going where there are children in both. Yet we were told of these secret relationships which were not 'flings' or 'one-night stands' but steady commitments over the years, with the claim that they did partially succeed.

Philip firmly believes that his choice of dual families is a sound basis for living:

PHILIP: *'I didn't want to divorce my first wife when I met and fell in love with Beth. I had read too much about what divorce can do to children. I made a decision: I would keep both families separate and provide in every sense of the word for both. And I do. I like to think our arrangement is all about being a new family. You will see more like me.'*

ANGUS: *'I am seen by work colleagues and family as a strong, honest guy. Yet for seven years I lived a double life with a wife and family in Doncaster and another 'wife' and kids in London. I can honestly say it did just happen. What I thought of as an affair became much, much more when Alice had a child. I don't believe anyone got hurt. It came to an end when Alice developed breast cancer. I knew then I had to be with her and Ben. That is when people got hurt. When I had to tell Jean and my boys. I knew I was right to have kept it secret. That way it was my responsibility and mine alone. Once it was in the open Jean and Alice both spoke of betrayal and of being misled. I never set out to mislead anyone. Now Jean is a single mother, I hardly see the boys and there is acrimony and recriminations all around. Even Alice and I are less compatible than we were.'*

How can there possibly be a happy ending in situations like these? Angus's view of his dual life may appear heroic and noble until it is realized that both 'wives' and all the children were (although perhaps unknowingly) forced into the deception of believing and living a lie. Death or disclosure still do not free the remaining family members from being part of a continuing deception.

The Children's Viewpoint

The *man* in each case was controlling the situation, with or without the collusion of the woman involved. There was a lack of acknowledgement that the family's existence was based on a lie and, most importantly, the feelings of the children were ignored. As we saw, Mark was caught up in the web of deceit spun by his father.

> MARK: *'I am sure Dad did not see it as deceit, but I do wonder how it all got started.'*

If a parent has a double life, it can have a serious effect on the children. We heard from Andrew, who was eleven when his parents divorced.

> ANDREW: *'My father left us and went to Australia. I remember that as a very bad time, my mother crying and we all felt so lost. We moved house and tried to get on with life. Three years later my dad came to visit and he and Mum seemed to make up. We all sat around whilst Dad told us – holding Mum's hand – that he was coming back. Well, not exactly. He put it to us that he had remarried and had a new baby. BUT he would be travelling between London and Sydney regularly and when here he would be our dad. My mother certainly agreed to it, and that was how it was. She would not discuss it ever, and my brother and I hated the idea. Dad even invited us to visit him one summer, so his "other" wife must have known too. I felt let down by my mum and dad and left home as soon as I could. I certainly blamed my mother as much as my father for creating the muddle. How could they DO it? I have never married. I don't think much of family life. Dad may have had a new family, we just had bits of the old one.'*

There are other circumstances in which a child has to cope with a parent's secret life. For instance, the media, and the public, were fascinated to know details about the hidden life, and family, of Bishop Roderick Wright. Kevin, fifteen years old, had always known who his father was, yet it was a secret that he had to keep. Finally, his mother, Ms Whibley, believed in all sincerity that it was only right that her son's father should be acknowledged publicly. This was no kiss-and-tell story: she felt Kevin had been profoundly hurt by being forced to live the same lie as his mother. She stated firmly that it had nothing to do with the public disclosure of Bishop Wright's 'other' secret life with a married woman. Yet, for years, she had kept silent whilst

Kevin's father had been involved with what she took to be his 'other' family: the Church. Kevin is quoted as saying, 'He might have been a good priest, but he was a rotten father.'

Another case came to light in 1996 when a man was sent to prison for bigamy. It set off a furore in the press where the debate was centred on speculation about the difficulties for a man in dividing his time and himself between two women. Not unusually, the press focused on the practical, particularly sexual, demands on the man, 'Think of the organization: grass to cut, bins to empty, two sets of in-laws, anniversaries to remember!' Again – as so often when divorce is treated by the media – it was the children and the effect on them that was ignored. Men in similar situations were interviewed and words such as 'randy' and a 'love rat' were used to describe them in grudging admiration. Not one article discussed their failure as fathers.

In order to maintain two lives a man needs stamina, for sure, and a good memory. But the factor which seems to be paramount is unfortunately a disregard for the feelings of others. Angus – whom we quoted earlier – might like to think he was 'protecting' both families by keeping them secret from each other, but he now freely admits that both Jean and Alice are suffering the intense pain of betrayal after disclosure. Angus felt that everyone got hurt when he told the truth. He found it incomprehensible that he might be responsible for the web of deceit and lies that he had spun over the years.

One can only guess what a complicated psychological profile there must be for the person who brings about these relationships: not only denial of the feelings of others, but of splitting off feelings for one family at a time, and projecting unwanted feelings on to members of the other family. Perhaps a feeling of omnipotence to be the one 'in the know' whilst the other family members are kept in the dark about the true situation.

There are no organizations to help with this sort of situation. Indeed, a call from Henry asking us how to untangle himself from a dual family situation left us no alternative but to urge him to seek professional counselling or therapy. He denied he needed help in that way and wanted practical help from us, a list of 'what to do' and 'how to do it'. He asked us if it were better to disappear or to tell both families about each other. Clearly the pressure had got too much for Henry to deal with and for him flight seemed an option.

We were left feeling concern for all the other 'Henrys', their 'wives' and, above all, the children of these families.

8   Second Weddings

So, a crisis, insoluble problem, major crisis, both stepmothers want
their names on the wedding invitation.

Yasmina Reza, *Art*

Till Death Do Us Part?

A wedding ceremony is the affirmation in public of the legal union of
two people. The most romantic of us see marriage as a contract. Some
form of wedding ceremony is part of the tradition of all societies. Most
people's parents were married and their parents before them. Marriage
is not a dying institution, in spite of highly publicized statistical data
used to prove otherwise; with the high rate of divorce marriage is still a
fashionable state. More than 291,000 marriages took place in 1994
(the latest year to provide statistics). Until comparatively recently, the
most common reason for a remarriage was death of a spouse. It was
not all that long ago that a woman's life was circumscribed first by
marriage, then by the birth of her children and finally her husband's
death. The decline of the adult mortality rate changed this pattern by
producing marriages of unprecedented length which in turn encouraged society to introduce the escape hatch of divorce. Marriages lasted
longest in the Victorian period when declining mortality rates had not
been offset by rising divorce rates.

The salient features of the marriage contract are the provision for
protection of property and the legitimizing of children. The latter does
not, unfortunately, ensure a child's health or well-being but is legally
binding only in giving the child his or her father's name and ongoing
financial support. So marriage has little to do with parenting in the
comprehensive way that is now implied.

In our society marriage is also an industry: many thousands of
pounds are spent every year on white dresses, multi-tiered cakes, hire
cars, flowers and presents in celebration of the joining of a couple. But
in the United States, because of the changing pattern of marriage in
recent years, couples are now being offered engagement and wedding
rings for hire, in case the relationship does not last: the rate of return
for engagement rings is currently 50 per cent! The owner of one large
chain of shops across the country says that in cases of heartache, 'our
staff are trained to demonstrate sensitivity'. After one year newlyweds

are sent a message of congratulations on surviving the year. This kind of attitude can only serve to promulgate the idea that marriage is temporary and can be terminated without difficulty or loss of any kind.

Everyone in Their Places

Nowadays four out of every ten weddings are second marriages for one or both of the partners. A new guide to wedding etiquette covers such issues as the social position of the divorcee, remarriage arrangements and advising that 'It remains good manners to inform any previous spouse as soon as possible of your intention to marry.' Second time around the convention is no longer for the father of the bride to pay for a wedding, particularly as the cost of a wedding soars each year. Indeed, the bridal couple often feel they would prefer to pay for their own wedding.

> ELLIE: 'My first wedding was paid for by Dad and planned to please Mum. This time I want the wedding to be just how I plan it; of course, Jack and I are paying for it all.'

A wedding is a hugely emotional affair first time around, but subsequent weddings where there are children from previous relationships can be especially fraught. So extra careful handling of the etiquette and organization of the ceremony is necessary. With a first-time traditional family wedding, everyone knows his or her place and specific role. The parents of the bride and the parents of the groom, even if they do not hit it off, can hopefully come together on that day. A second wedding is more complex; the mixture of key players can cause problems: it is not all that unusual for there to be a mix of the bride's parents and her siblings plus children from her first marriage, possibly with the same amalgam from the groom's side.

> BERYL: 'I'd call it a minefield. There are so many different people to consider.'

And it can be a lot more convoluted than this:

> ANDY: 'It was even more complicated for us. I wanted my stepdaughter from my first marriage to be at the wedding, and the children I had with my bride-to-be. She also had three children from a previous marriage, so it took some managing. My mother

wasn't speaking to my new in-laws and then the grandparents of
my stepdaughter wanted to be present at the ceremony too.'

SALLY: *'My goodness, the complications at our wedding. There*
were my children, his children, and our children. It is difficult
enough to arrange a straightforward bride's family's side, and
groom's side, but where do you put the combination we had?'

Andrea gave careful thought to her second marriage, and decided it
was not possible to follow the usual pattern:

ANDREA: *'We greeted everyone ourselves and said, "Sit where you*
like for the ceremony." When the photographer came he gave up
trying to organize us and we have some lovely spontaneous photos
which really show the families merging together.'

The relaxed attitude of Andrea and her husband, Peter, helped to
smooth the path. They were unconcerned about appearances and
wanted their loved ones around them, as Peter said, 'in any combination'. Deborah's situation was the opposite: she admits little thought
went into planning where people would sit and stand:

DEBORAH: *'When the photographer said, "Father of the bride here,*
please," we all froze. It was my mum who came to the rescue and
told my stepfather to stand next to me and my real dad to go next to
my husband's mother.'

One look at the photographs shows the strain on their faces, and
reinforces the convictions that thought and consideration must be
given to all the players in this game – otherwise there is no protection
from embarrassment and discomfort.

The speeches, too, can cause a problem. When Alice, at the age of
thirty-four, married for the second time, she and Sam decided to keep
the affair simple and informal. They told her father, whom she had
seen only infrequently since her parents' divorce, that this was what
they wanted, and there was to be no proud father-of-the-bride speech.

ALICE: *'After all, he had done it once before.'*

However, at the moment of cutting the cake Alice's stepfather rose to
his feet and spoke at length of his pride in having Alice as his
daughter. Alice was horrified, Sam was angry, Alice's father was hurt,
and the mother-of-the-bride was in tears.

ALICE: *'Do make it clear to everyone just what you want and don't want them to do.'*

Ex-partners and their Children

A stepfamily wedding can be a painful reminder of the first family and the breakup that ensued. This is particularly hard if there was a death, or if the split was very recent and emotions are still raging high. It may also be the bringing together of two groups of children who do not want to be merged. The wedding day itself can stir up old arguments and rock the fragile foundations on which hopes for the future have been pinned. It is not the time to have deep discussions or the moment to reconsider arrangements about whom the children should live with.

Feelings not dealt with up until then or hidden away for years may surface at this time, and past arguments be refuelled. Different family members will have their own opinions and thoughts about the wedding and it is impossible to please everyone. A feeling of being caught between them all is not a good way to start anew. Fortunately, some couples can put the feeling of failure behind them and see the wedding as a marker for their future together.

Because a wedding is a time for looking forward, remarrying is a fresh beginning, not just for the new couple but for all the children, resident and non-resident, of each partner. It is important not to ignore or belittle the earlier marriages or partnerships; since these relationships are responsible for the children's existence, they must always be seen in a positive light in front of them: you cannot wipe out the past.

> JACKIE: *'Despite it being seven years after my divorce, it was still a shock to me to hear that my ex-husband was remarrying. Our children, all under ten, did not think it any big deal because his new wife Lucy had been living with their dad for five years and they had two daughters together, and as far as they were concerned the relationship was permanent. For very young children the fact of being or not being married is not the issue, it is more the commitment they see, of the living together.'*

This was echoed by Mavis who also believes that very young children cannot appreciate or understand the importance of a wedding service, especially if the couple have been living together for many years. The visible act of being a couple is what is important to a young child. All this is very confusing for younger children, and their questions need to be listened to and answered.

LOUISE, aged six, confused by the news of her father's imminent wedding: '*I thought you had to be married before you went to bed together.*'

GEORGE, aged seven, when told his father and partner were going to be married, was puzzled and said: '*But I thought you had been married to Sheila since you left us.*'

AUDREY: '*It was the week of my ex's remarriage and Peter was ten when we had this conversation. "Will you read me some of my school book?", he asked. Suspecting that something else was in the back of his mind I asked, "Why?" He said, "Oh please, you'll be my best mum." I replied that I was his only mother. But Peter reminded me that he also had a stepmum now. I gasped with hurt and shock as I replied calmly that it was not a competition and left the room. Later I wondered if perhaps I had overreacted about a cheeky comment because of my own feelings about the marriage?*'

To marry without a parent's consent is one thing, but to remarry without the support of your dependent children, especially if they live with you, needs to be handled with kid gloves to avoid disaster and long-term ill effects.

PETRA: '*My mum and Gordon called me in one day and said they wanted to get married, but only if I agreed. As Gordon had lived with us for two years, I couldn't see the point. Why ask me? It made me feel resentful and when I said I didn't mind I felt I was letting my dad down.*'

The decision to remarry or not cannot be taken lightly and the effect on others, particularly the children, must be given full weight.

PAULA: '*The man I'm seeing has custody of his three children, and I have shared custody of my two. If we didn't have children, I think we wouldn't hesitate about getting married. But when we contemplate the issues involved in putting all these people together, it's absolutely daunting.*'

CILLA: '*I knew why I was remarrying. Rightly or wrongly, who was to say? But I enjoyed being married. I felt I needed the security and protection of the status, and I have this great fear of being alone. I thought that if I felt good I would be a better mother to the children. I couldn't understand why they resented Derek so much. He wasn't an ideal father figure but he was there.'*

MAGGIE: *'I am hoping to marry James within the next few months, but only if we can secure my capital and property as my own, with no claim on it from his ex-wife, now or in the future. I am forty-one and have worked hard for what I have. If things don't work out I will not put myself in the position of losing it all.'*

JENNY: *'After Pete left I had several long-term relationships. All my partners became very involved in the children and all aspects of our lives. After a few years, my son Tim, aged ten, said to me that he was getting fed up with the constant changes of half- dads and of getting to know all these men and having them leave. So could I just decide on one, marry him and then we could all get on with our lives in a settled way. I was a fool for listening to a ten-year-old, because six months after marrying David it all fell apart and we are all terribly bruised.'*

VICKY: *'I always liked the same kind of man and after three marriages, all of which produced children, and three divorces I thought it was time to rethink my life. Perhaps the kind of husbands I chose were not the settling down kind? When Mark and I fell in love I knew that he was as solid as a rock and ideal husband material. We married and were very happy for several years, only he was fifteen years older than me and became very ill and bedridden. That in itself put a different kind of burden on me and the marriage. Not at all what I had hoped for.'*

BERNESE: *'I would have married Eddie years earlier if the children had liked him, but I went on with my "caught in the middle" life for seven years because I thought that was preferable for all concerned, rather than to have us all together as one unhappy merged family. When the children were teenagers and my eldest had gone off to college, we did get married and everyone accepted it and they seem happy enough. I will never know if it's because of how we did it or if I should have just got on with what I wanted seven years ago.'*

Children at their Parents' Second Weddings

If it is the resident parent who remarries, the children will sense something in the air and it is likely that they will get in the right frame of mind to accept the significance of the wedding occasion. On the other hand, if it is the non-custodial parent, especially if he or she is cohabiting, it may be more difficult for the children to understand the importance of the wedding. So it is the non-custodial parent with his or her new partner who may decide against inviting the children.

JANICE: '*I was furious when my ex telephoned me three days before his wedding to tell me of his plans. How could he not prepare the children? Why did he not want to include them? Why get married midweek when the children are in school? How was it possible that he hadn't thought of his children at a time which is so important? I felt sick with worry. Should I tell them? And if so how?*'

Fiona's story was similar:

FIONA: '*My three children (four, seven and eight years) were told four weeks before the event that their dad was remarrying. It was, my ex said, "too difficult to organize for them to come out of school on a Wednesday and that they all thought it for the best if the children didn't go". So they didn't. I found this very difficult to accept and in the days leading up to the wedding the children were very aggressive and angry with everyone and everything, yoyoing with outbursts of tears and screaming. Then literally the evening after the wedding, all seemed calmer and back to normal. When I put James (eight) to bed that night, he said to me that he was glad it was all over now!*'

SERENA: '*My ex didn't tell the kids in advance that he was getting married. Both the boys (eleven and fourteen) were upset that they hadn't been included and I heard the younger one telling his brother that when he got married he wouldn't invite his dad and then he could see what it was like to feel this way. How very sad. I realized that we had a great deal of ground to cover to help him to accept what had happened and not to build a problem for the future now, a resolution that he felt at a later date he could not break.*'

MADDY: '*It was left up to me to tell my twelve-year-old that his father had remarried. James said, "It's just as well I wasn't invited, I would have pushed Catherine out of the way if I had seen Dad putting a ring on her finger." He was all bluster to cover up his hurt, I think. Next day he said to me, "Catherine has ruined my life." I was quick to say, "Catherine has changed your life, but only you can let her ruin it."*'

JOAN: *'My siblings and I were left out of my dad's second wedding, and it still bugs us twenty-four years later. He gave some stupid reason for not even telling us it was happening, and claims he didn't want my mother to know about the event, so he didn't invite us. We found out after they got back from their honeymoon.'*

Joan shows how events that are handled without much forethought can still rankle many years later. Joan went on to tell us how being excluded from this important day in her father's life meant that for her and her siblings their relationship with their father and his wife was always uncomfortable and tinged with resentment. The hurt can be perpetuated as Serena fears with her son.

NANCY: *'I was not included in my mum's second, third, or fourth weddings. Years after the last wedding I asked her why I had never been included and she had no answer. Just looked at me as if I was foolish to ask the question. To anyone wanting to know what to do when getting remarried, I'd say to include all the children in some part of the occasion.'*

LUCY: *'Excluded? I'll say I was. The first I knew was a postcard from my dad saying "Guess what? I'm on my honeymoon."'*

MIRI: *'Invited to Dad's wedding – you must be joking. I heard of it when his wife rang up my mother and said their wedding photograph was in the local paper.'*

For Frank the answer seemed straightforward:

FRANK: *'When I married Lucy, it was a big affair. I asked my daughters if they wanted to be bridesmaids. The eldest jumped at it, but the youngest refused. Okay she came round in the end and "allowed" herself to be brought to the reception.'*

Some children identify with the feelings of their resident parent, though it is sometimes contrary to what they feel themselves. Children do pick up undercurrents of feeling and may not always interpret the situation correctly. A child would perhaps like to be at his (or her) father's wedding, but thinks that if he says this it will hurt the parent the child lives with. Or perhaps the children would like to go to the wedding but don't get on with their parent's new partner, and feel that to participate would be seen to accept a stepparent that they don't like. All these options need to be considered.

RACHEL: *'My daughter was seven when her dad remarried, and about the wedding she had said, "Half of me wanted to go and half of me didn't", and I think this showed how confusing her feelings were over the final commitment of her dad to the girl he was living with who Jenny didn't like.'*

When there is the news that one parent is about to remarry all hopes and fantasies that their mother and father will – against all the evidence – get back together again, are crushed.

KATIE (eight years old) asked her mother many questions around the time of her father's remarriage: *'What will Patty be to me? What will Daddy be to me? What will their baby be to me? Where will everyone live after the wedding?'*

When Sue answered as straightforwardly as possible Katie replied: 'Oh so nothing will be changed or different then!' Her relief was unbelievable.

Children see the world as revolving round themselves, and news of a wedding of a parent will bring up again such questions as what will happen to me? How will it be different for me? More questions that need to be heard and answered. Katie's questions showed that explanations need to be updated, and anxieties about what it all means need to be addressed.

Many people who spoke to us said that if the children wanted to be at the wedding they should be, but not if they didn't want to. Their minds should not be made up for them. But this is not as easy to put into practice as it sounds, especially when the children are young or unsure. Many questions and uncertainties were raised. What if one child does not want to go to the wedding and the other does but dares not say so?

SUSIE (a stepmother): *'My partner's five-year-old child did not come to our wedding. I'm not sure she was even told about it, anyway her mum would never have allowed her to come.'*

After hearing this it did not surprise us when Susie went on to say that she and her stepdaughter have never formed a comfortable relationship.

Margaret had been fortunate to have had counselling for herself and her three children ever since the split of their family three years before her ex-husband remarried:

MARGARET: *'My children took the separation from their father very badly and their hurt was very deep. Every time the children appeared to be on an even keel, they were forced to accept another change in their lives: moving house, having to change schools, new childminders to cover my return to work together with their father having three babies in quick succession. The latest upset was when their father married his girlfriend and they were not invited. My counsellor was horrified and said it was tragic they hadn't been included, and that it was very bad for the long-term acceptance of their stepmother, the fact that the children had not "actually witnessed the marriage".'*

Catherine also had the additional support of a child psychologist for her twin girls of nine. After they had been excluded from their father's wedding ceremony, they had started to act in a very childish way, shouting, getting hurt all the time and crying for attention. It was suggested to Catherine that she get the girls to draw pictures of how they thought the wedding had been, so when they did eventually see photographs, they could see if their ideas matched up. It also helped the children to focus on an external idea rather than bottling up all the confused feelings with no outlet except disruptive ones.

JACKIE: *'Tom was eleven when his father remarried. The night before the wedding, which Tom was not invited to, he closed his eyes, put his head in my lap and covered it with his arms. I asked what he was doing? The muffled reply was, "I want to hide in here with my face in the dark because I don't want Dad to get married. Here I can pretend it isn't happening, I will come out tomorrow and then it will be all gone."'*

Some children want or need to talk about what is happening in other parts of their lives, and others will bury it.

LUCY, aged eight: *'In school I told Mrs Butts that my daddy was getting married today and she asked me what was the name of daddy's friend and what was she like.'*

Hearing this her brother, fourteen, said, 'Well I didn't tell anyone anything.'

Fiona – whom we have heard from earlier – asked us if perhaps she should have done more at the time to help to get the situation sorted out: to see if the children did in fact want to go to their father's wedding. And if so, should she have tried to get them invited, despite her suspicions that it was her ex's new woman who didn't want the children there, so as not to mar her big day.

As always each family is different and the individuals within it must strive to find the right way to cope with each emotional or practical hurdle. There is not just one right way. One solution can never suit everyone. Also, there are inevitably two schools of thought: one for the original family and one for the new. We are primarily concerned with the children's thoughts and reactions and what is best for them, and to extend our understanding of what makes a successful family.

It is always best to be aware of these situations before being caught unawares, so it is of great value to know how others found a solution. One of the reasons why merged families have more than their share of burdens is partly because there are children from more than one relationship and trying to balance the priorities for all the children may still result in someone being hurt, and quite possibly everyone. This is particularly sad when the intentions have been good.

> DAVID: *'I will never understand my dad. I felt okay about his wedding, until he asked my brother to be his best man. In the end, I didn't go to the wedding, and hardly ever see them.'*

There can be religious reasons for a child not being at a parent's remarriage, as in the case of Sarah:

> SARAH: *'We did not let Sam, our stepson, come to our wedding because according to Jewish law, a child is not supposed to see the marriage of a parent. This was okay for Sam until his mother remarried and she had him at hers, and only then did he feel he had been excluded from ours.'*

> CHRISTY: *'I was not included in either my mum's second or subsequent weddings. Her second wedding was a grand affair, her third more modest – but there was no role for me at either. Please tell everyone to include all their children in some part of the occasion.'*

How about when children do not invite one of their parents to their wedding?

> ELIZABETH: *'My parents divorced when I was three years old and I had little contact with my father for most of my life. When I married at nineteen I didn't invite him to my wedding and I didn't feel any regret. My stepfather gave me away, as he was my "dad". But when my son was born, two years later, it changed my whole*

perspective on all my parents. I re-established contact with my father and realized how it could have been different. I really do regret the fact I didn't make an effort to invite him.'

Wedding exclusions do not stop with age either: Deborah, thirty-nine, told us that her father remarried and although she and her husband went, her children were not invited. It was her children, aged twelve and fifteen, who asked in astonishment why they also couldn't go to their grandpa's wedding. Deborah, herself, isn't clear either but felt it was more to do with her stepmother's feelings than her father's.

DEBORAH: *'How could I tell them they weren't wanted there, who knows why? All I can say is it hasn't helped us to rebuild a family.'*

For older children, too, a parent's subsequent marriage may cause heartache:

YVONNE: *'Divorce in my family killed my mother. A year after Dad left us she took an overdose of pills. I could hardly be expected to dance at my father's wedding. But I am an adult, and I put on a civilized face on the day. I kept the tears for home.'*

Matilda recalled how her two stepchildren-to-be cast a cloud over her wedding day:

MATILDA: *'The girls were six and seven and Ronald wanted them there. I didn't want them to be bridesmaids, but it was okay by me if they wanted to be present. I hadn't bargained on them making a fuss. Firstly through the ceremony and then at the reception. They became very babyish, crying and wanting their dad to carry them, for heaven's sake! Our photos were ruined by them hanging on to his legs and refusing to stand still.'*

Greg also reported a fiasco on his wedding day. He feels he cannot forgive his stepchildren for the pain they caused that day.

GREG: *'I thought Marie's kids – teenagers – would behave. In fact they came in a sullen, sulky mood. They refused to tidy themselves up and looked like down-and-outs. Even worse was their attitude. They mooned around and wouldn't celebrate. At the speeches Lily started to cry and ran from the reception. I'm sure she timed it like that. It upset a lot of people and Marie was distraught. That's what they wanted I suppose. I won't forgive them in a hurry.'*

These two very distressing memories do emphasize the point that family discussions must take place beforehand, so feelings can be aired and consequences thought about.

> PHYLLIS: *'When I remarried I included my three-year-old daughter in the wedding. She remembers it clearly and often mentions it now – she is nine. However my ex remarried last month and didn't include her and she was very very hurt. He told her they will have a public celebration some time in the spring, but I think it will always be in her thoughts that she was left out of the actual day. Especially as she knows how much she enjoyed being a special part of my big day.'*

The ceremony was an equally difficult occasion for Lucy, when her mother remarried. Lucy, now thirty-seven, told us that she was twelve when her mother announced that she was remarrying.

> LUCY: *'I thought Mum would have a white wedding and that I could be a bridesmaid, but I was wrong. I was furious and even now I can't picture Mum on her wedding day, perhaps I didn't look. I just remember me and my brother sitting in the front pew and her going off to sign the register. "Going off" I suppose and leaving me and my brother, that's what stuck in my mind. I always thought of my stepfather as temporary and I was right, that marriage only lasted four years.'*

Happier Solutions

Several parents told us that they arranged for a favourite aunt or friend to 'shadow' a son or daughter through the actual wedding day. Someone to keep a special eye on the child in case there were upsets or in case a child felt left out. And we did in fact receive many happy stories of successful second weddings where children had merged in without problems and the day had been a joyous occasion.

> MARY: *'A friend of mine had her two daughters as maids of honour at her second wedding. Her husband-to-be gave each of the girls a special ring during the ceremony. They were eleven and fourteen years old.'*

> VICTORIA: *'When I got married again, my son, aged ten, was the "best man". He asked for a ring too, and my husband, luckily a dentist, made him one out of dental gold.'*

ANNIE: *'I brought up Natalie on my own and when I met my now husband I knew he'd be a wonderful father for my daughter. I felt he'd be an example of the best male role you could have. We wanted "our" daughter to be included in the wedding and we wanted to have the ceremony reflect that we were uniting as a family. Natalie came up with this idea: she made a necklace and at one point in the ceremony my husband fastened the necklace on her while the minister talked about the necklace being a symbol of our joining together as a family. It meant a lot to Natalie. She often talks about how "we" got married.'*

Now that the regulations about where couples can be married have been extended there is more scope for planning weddings with a difference. This can be particularly helpful when combining two families with children: they can be included in ways not so easy when the only choice was a traditional or civil ceremony.

VERA: *'My husband and I got married last July and we each have two children from previous marriages. We decided to make it a children-friendly ceremony because we wanted our children to feel included and because we had several young nieces and nephews who would also attend. We had the ceremony outside and our four young children sat at our feet blowing bubbles during the vows, that wasn't exactly how we planned it, but it actually ended up being very memorable. After the ceremony we filled up two paddling pools with water and let the children splash while the adults enjoyed a catered meal. Everyone who attended said it was the most unique and stress-free wedding they'd ever experienced. My husband and I were so very glad we ignored the advice of well-meaning relatives and went ahead with our unorthodox plans. Our combined family is doing very, very well. We had a good start by including the children in the special day. We wanted them to understand that we were combining two families to make a whole.'*

JANE: *'I got remarried and we have five children ranging from seven years to sixteen. They were at our wedding and we all lit the unity candle together. My kids were happy because it was a new start for them. We'd had a sad period because my first husband died from cancer. My new husband's kids were very confused for a long time because they hadn't wanted their parents to get divorced. The wedding ceremony was the beginning of a new start for us all. We felt a family at last.'*

JACK: *'We compromised. On the Saturday we made it Gerri's day –
white dress, the lot. On the Sunday I had my kids and we had a
kind of family blessing of the union which included them, and
made us a family I hope.'*

Joanna was adamant that the presence of the children is an integral
part of the wedding ceremony and they must be seen to have a specific
role to enable them to feel part of it all.

JOANNA: *'When Martin and I were married the boys were eight and
twelve. One was the candle-lighter and the other was the ring-
carrier. When the priest asked "Who gives this woman?" both the
boys said, "We do." It was great fun and they had a really good
time. The boys helped in the planning of the wedding and the
holiday activities, so felt they were really a part of all things. As a
result they were very supportive of the marriage and now they are
sixteen and fourteen they still are.'*

PAULA: *'When Rob and I married we both wanted to involve his
children (Ben, aged five, Sarah, aged six, and Jane, aged eight) as
much as possible (their mother had died four years before). We
followed our marriage ceremony with a family blessing service
and felt it was a very important day for us ALL. ... As soon as the
wedding was over the children called me Mummy, and the girls
told their teachers that it was lovely to call someone that again.'*

JULIE: *'When my wedding was being planned I had to decide who
was to give me away. Not my dad who I had only seen once a year
for the past sixteen years, and not my mother's new husband who I
had never lived with. I had no older brothers or male cousins. In
the end I asked Mum to give me away because she is the most
important person in my life and it seems right that she hands me
over to Brian. She was thrilled.'*

POLLY: *'I just couldn't decide who should give me away, because
dad and I had a fairly good relationship especially since he returned
to England last year. However, it was Ron who had given me the
love and support of family life with mum. In the end I thought it
would spoil the day if I made the wrong choice so I asked them if
they would mind standing either side of me and for us all to walk
down the isle together. It worked.'*

LUCY: *'When I got married to Paul my girls were thirteen and fourteen years old. Both my parents are dead. I had both of the girls walk me down the aisle and when the preacher said "Who gives this woman to this man?" they said "We do."'*

A second wedding can add meaning to the phrase 'family wedding'. Whereas traditionally the principal players were always the parents of both the bride and the groom and the young couple, it is now often the beginning of the formal reconstruction of a family.

PAULINE: *'I have two kids from my previous marriage, and John has one son. You go into a second marriage with the intention of not making the same mistakes again only to find out that the second wedding has a completely new set of rules. Still, sorting it all out brought us all closer together. We all spoke of "our" wedding.'*

TONY: *'These are interesting times for us all. We're all having to redefine the word "family" since our marriage. It can mean so many things these days, but the bottom line is that they nearly always mean a little group of people somehow connected who really make life worth living, and who provide the confidence to go out and live in the world.'*

The Problem of Names

The spectre of the first spouse can linger over many second weddings.

JANICE: *'I kept my own name. I didn't want to be known as the second Mrs X.'*

This question of names can be especially important for the children. When Marie told her children of six and nine that she was marrying Neal, her son's only comment was, 'Will I have to change my name?' Susie told us a similar story:

SUSIE: *'After I had been dating Ed for several months my son of eight asked me what Ed's surname was. I told him and his comment was, "Oh, no I don't want that name as mine" which alerted me to the fact that he was contemplating me marrying again. I left this for a few days and then said to Jeremy that I had no plans to get married and that if I did he would be the first person I would talk to, so he was not even to think about it at the moment as it was not on the cards.'*

JACK: *'My name is Bond and when we decided to get married I assumed Jenny's kids would take my name. No way – and the revolt was led by James who is fifteen. Once I realized why, all we could do was laugh.'*

MAVIS: *'I decided to keep my married name but add a hyphen with my new name. That way I felt it formed a bridge for his and my kids and the kids we had together.'*

CONNIE: *'Funny things, names. A woman marries and she takes her husband's name. Poof, a marriage and it's done. Then a woman gets divorced, and it is hard to "undo" the married name – kinda like "undoing" the marriage, I suppose.'*

STACY: *'I didn't want to repeat the same vows he and his first wife had said. "Till death do us part" is a nonsense, especially now, so we devised our own ceremony vows, and I didn't change my name.'*

ROSE: *'When I divorced my ex I kept his name because of our son. My husband's first wife also kept his name. Oh well, she had his name for twenty-six years. Old habits die hard.'*

Others had firmer views about whether the children should change their name.

DOT: *'Certainly not, they are who they are as a result of my union with my first husband. He is still their father, and they have his name.'*

BECKY: *'When I married Simon, I changed my name to his because we knew we would have a baby together, but we left my children's name as it was in memory of their dad who died.'*

ROBERT: *'No real worries about names – my new wife took mine. There were more difficulties about what the children would call me. They knew me as Rob and on our wedding day I asked them to change to Dad. One did, one didn't.'*

VINCE: *'There were no real problems; we took everything slowly, the children moved from referring to me as "mummy's friend" to "daddy" after the wedding. It wouldn't have been right before.'*

HUGH: *'They were four and seven years old when I entered their lives.*

By six and nine years old they had outgrown "Daddy Hughey" and called me "Dad". The only real problem was from their biological father and his intense jealousy that I was being the kids' "dad".'

The Honeymoon

Should the usual honeymoon period after a wedding be just for two, or, when there are children, for three or more? Over the years the concept of a honeymoon has changed. Originally it was a description of the first weeks after marriage. Next it became a time of travel, but in the company of others; it was not unusual for the couple to be accompanied by bridesmaids or other companions. It is only comparatively recently that the time after a marriage has been seen as a special time for the couple to have some privacy in which to explore each other. However, in the age of remarriage, when children from previous relationships have to be taken into account, a honeymoon can be celebrated in a variety of ways.

FRANCES: *'My children were very much a part of our wedding and then they stayed the weekend with their grandma so we could get away by ourselves, and then the following week we all went away together.'*

LEE: *'When I married Bill, I gave all the important roles to my boys. After the wedding my sister took them for a couple of days so that we had time alone, and then we all took a trip together for a couple more days. Not a traditional honeymoon, but having them with us cemented our new family.'*

SAM: *'When Jenny and I got married we both had a child from our first marriage. We went without the children on a two-week trip because as we explained to the children it was our celebration of the union. When we got home, we took the children away to Euro Disney for the weekend and explained to them that this was their celebration of it. They were both exactly the same age and by the end of the weekend they had decided to tell everyone that they were twins. Unfortunately this did not turn out to be such a good idea because my daughter had to go back and live with her mum, and for us that was a worse problem than if we were a whole stepfamily all the time.'*

MATTHEW: *'When we married, Jo already had a daughter and to be honest I didn't want her with us on our honeymoon. But I kept quiet and we made the best of it because I realized that by loving and committing myself to Jo, I have to do the same for Lucy and although it's not always easy I accept my responsibilities. After all Jo was a mother when I met her and it was no good saying to her that she had to pretend to me otherwise just because we were on a honeymoon. Her parents have promised us the chance of a weekend away in the spring and I'm looking forward to that.'*

Peter was not so clear in his thinking and told us that he wished he had thought it through more before the trouble really began. He had put his foot down at taking his new wife's children on their honeymoon. It was the start of many years of hurt and anger. Now they are two years on but still the boys, aged twelve and nine, talk about 'the holiday when we left them behind'.

Family Unity

So a wedding, which should be a joyous occasion, can all too easily introduce stormy weather for all concerned when it is a second wedding. Validation must be given to the different feelings generated by the news, and they are often likely to be mixed. Yet it is helpful in the long run to consider these feelings from all sides. If a couple have been living under the same roof, it is still a fresh landmark. For many children it is the final piece of information which takes away any hope, conscious or unconscious, that their parents will get back together again. For other family members – particularly parents – they may still have loving feelings towards an ex-son- or daughter-in-law which are not in step with the new bridal couple.

If a couple have truly divorced 'emotionally' it is possible to be pleased that an ex-spouse has found happiness. While feelings of betrayal or anger are alive, it is not easy to be generous if an ex-partner finds happiness. But time does heal, and Sue felt a burst of generosity and love towards Bill when he met and married Angie.

SUE: *'Bill is a lovely man – and I can honestly say I wish him well.'*

Complications are more likely to be rife if children are in the picture. Refreshingly, we heard from Patricia:

PATRICIA: *'My ex-husband remarried twelve years after we divorced. By then all the hate and recriminations were over. Me and my husband were thrilled to be at his wedding and to wish him and his bride well for their future together. It helped that the children had become very fond of his new wife and I could see no strain there – we could all celebrate together. No one was hurting any more at last.'*

It is not easy to celebrate when there is still mourning unresolved. For example, if either the bride or groom are themselves from a divorced family, it can be one more time when, perhaps unexpectedly, stress runs high as old wounds are reopened. It may also be a time when parents and a new partner are thrown together with a former wife or husband who himself may not have a new spouse, and this can bring about unforseen difficulties:

ANDREA: *'My husband and I felt outnumbered at our wedding! We both have divorced parents, and all four have remarried. Think of that – think of the undercurrents.'*

On the other hand if the remarriage is hotfoot upon a divorce, the pain of seeing a loved one moving on to a new choice can be hurtful indeed, above all for the children. Many issues affect the children's reaction to the news of a parent's remarriage and the timing is always an important factor, the moment at which the permanence of a stepparent is affirmed by marriage perhaps more than anything else. In Chapter 4 we discussed the importance of preparing a child to accept a new parent and how it is necessary to stress that the new wife or husband is not replacing the child's other real parent. This cannot be underestimated and this concern often rises to the surface again around the time of a new wedding.

And there is another element in all of this which must not be overlooked. We must spare a thought for the new groom or bride for whom this may be a first wedding! As we heard from Jack: on the Saturday the focus was solely on his new bride, and the emphasis did not change until the next day with a family blessing which encompassed them all.

It always adds up to the same thing: the necessity of careful preparation beforehand. The news of a marriage should not be broken to the children without consultation and discussion with all the adults, especially the other parent. Frequently, it is the resident parents who have to cope with most of the upset and upheaval, partly because they are the ones who are there and partly because for every situation which comes out into the open there are bound to be unconscious repercussions which need recognizing and dealing with. Children will sometimes appear not to react at the time the problem originates, especially if they are with the non-custodial parent; perhaps they don't want to spoil the moment. The problems are often addressed once they are back home. Once more, the emphasis is on discussion and an agreement about what and when to tell children important news which will certainly affect them profoundly.

The new regulations regarding where couples may now marry has enabled some couples to be quite inventive, by including children in a less orthodox way.

> TONY: 'We had a civil ceremony in the morning, but in the afternoon a blessing in our garden. All the children were fully involved in the planning. Each made a contribution. One suggested handing out popcorn, and we all combined ideas to make a lovely family day.'

It is hard when a discussion has taken place with the children's benefit in mind and it is all undone by an ex-partner's careless words. After a remarriage this can be compounded by the opinion of the new partner too. Careful handling must continue so as not to confuse the children, and it is not a healthy situation if no one knows who has the last word. The children will need to know if there are any additional rules or changes that will affect their lives. A wedding *is* a landmark in any family and those adults and children who have been burned by the fallout of an earlier divorce will be particularly sensitive to the meaning of the occasion. With some planning, and a lot of discussion, and a little luck it can still become a day memories are made of:

> IRIS: 'As Charles and I got up to cut the cake I saw the expression on the faces of my son and Charles's little girl. As one, we beckoned them forward and those eight hands clasped together made a wonderful photograph and a strong start to our new family.'

9   Alternative Decisions

L'embarras des richesses.

[The more alternatives, the more difficult the choice.]

Abbé d'Allainval

The Childless Family

A growing number of couples are making the decision not to have children. For some, it may be a lifestyle preference and may not mean they do not like children. Others may have tried to have children in the past, but then aimed to live a contented married life without becoming parents. Some just do not want children.

In the United Kingdom the British Organization of Non-Parents (BON) is just twenty years old, and it tries to represent the view of the voluntarily child-free. The organization sees itself as the consistent and articulate voice for 'elective non-parents'. Language is something of a problem – there is no word for 'deciding not to have a child' – therefore because the majority of couples are parents, BON has had to become an organization for 'non-parents'. This projects a more negative view than they would like to present and their twentieth-anniversary newsletter issued in January 1998 announces with loud acclaim that, 'Those who choose not to have children are not a threat, but are rather different but equal.'

Couples who do decide not to have children find themselves on the receiving end of advice, questions, and enquiries from well-meaning friends and relations. They are told 'You don't know your own minds', 'You'll be sorry', or are even asked 'What about your old age?'

KATE: *'As if a good reason for having children is an insurance for later years.'*

ANGELA: *'The answer I give when somebody says "When are you two going to have a baby?" is "When you learn some manners."'*

JOHN: *'Why is it that people feel they have the right to ask really intimate questions?'*

ROOT CARTWRIGHT, the founder of BON: *'People do have a cheek. Perfect strangers seem to feel they have the right to ask why you don't have children. I turn the tables and ask, "Why do you have children?" They soon bluster away.'*

ROBERT: *'It took a time to decide. What held us back for some time was the unspoken family pressure. I felt the pressure to reproduce, to carry on the family name. But I wanted time to grow, to mature myself before attempting to teach another human how to be. The deadline neared, and by then I was secure in who I am and knew what mattered to us as a couple.'*

Those couples who spoke to us said they felt they were given no credit for the thought and consideration they put into their decision not to have children.

ROOT: *'A lot of self-examination goes on before such an important decision is made. I know from our members they are not glib or feckless and much self-searching goes on beforehand.'*

JANEY: *'We are getting married in June and I am having tubal ligation in April. The snip before the wedding makes it entirely clear I am not going to change my mind.'*

SAM: *'We knew how we felt, but it was still an agonizing time, going against the tide, you see.'*

REBECCA: *'It was not a snap decision, believe me. I had to confront thoughts I had kept hidden from myself. Was I sick? Was I deranged? Did I not love my fiance enough? Doesn't everybody want children? Well, no. I made peace with myself and it took time. I tell my story now so others may also find peace within themselves, as I did.'*

ROBERT: *'We thought we would "let time decide". That is if we didn't have a child by accident – despite our efforts at prevention. We would see how we felt by, say, forty.'*

Child-free

Although for many couples choosing not to have children is *not* the same as disliking them, this is not always so:

TOM: *'Well, it seems I have always disliked kids, even when I was one. I enjoy my freedom.'*

MARIA: *'I do not want children. I have seen more than enough of children's cruelty. I hated being a child.'*

Some who saw the pain of their parents *being* parents have made their choice because of this:

SARAH: *'I feel uneasy around children, and I was happy to be sterilized, and not have to worry any more. It means I will never be my alcoholic stuck-at-home mother. It means I will never be my father, who hated to come home to an alcoholic stuck-at-home wife and all the children he had to provide for.'*

PAUL: *'My mother ended up depressed and suicidal. I used to blame her for it. I don't any longer. I blame parenthood for ruining what might have been a productive, joyful life for her. I won't have children of my own.'*

Perhaps too many people drift into being parents, and although for some, this can be the beginning of a happy family life, it can bring about disastrous consequences both for the couple, and for the child.

ROBERT: *'I spoke with both child-free people and parents. I discovered many parents remain ambivalent about their children. Several couples told me that if they had their time over again they would choose not to have children.'*

Robert told us that he got the impression from different people that most of their children were 'accidents' and conceived with little thought about what they were doing, or why.

Child-free partners, as we have seen, are often called upon to *justify* their decision of why they have chosen to remain childless. However, such couples are becoming more vocal and want to contradict those who see them as unfulfilled, or at worst, ambitious, selfish or self-centred. They are no longer a silent minority. Like the one-parent family, or the stepfamily, the childless family is becoming a recognized unit in society. But child-free women spoke of the hostility they received from other women. 'It's as if we haven't joined the club.' There is often an aura of 'You'll be sorry' around, and a sense that the side has been let down, and a punishment will surely follow at some time. This is the impression given by Austria's Family Minister (as reported in the *Guardian*, 20 February 1997) who has called for the retirement age for childless women to be raised. His announcement follows pleas to the country's women to have more children. The Minister says it is not his intention to punish childless women, yet it is difficult to see it in any other way.

On the Internet there are forums for couples who do not want children to be in contact with each other. Candace Korasick, who started the web site Childfree in 1997, told us:

> CANDACE KORASICK: 'When I started mentioning to people that my husband and I were considering not having children most of my friends and co-workers were adamantly opposed. "You're too young to make that sort of decision." I stopped discussing it with anyone but my husband. I finally told my mother, and, just as I suspected, she was very supportive. Now I have a network of people who support my chosen lifestyle, but I can't forget the year I spent thinking that I must be defective. That's why I started Childfree.'

In the United States Childless by Choice also speaks for the men and women who have made, or are in the process of making, this decision.

> CARIN: 'We focus on literature and information for people without kids, and deal with the press. We like to provide couples with answers to the questions fired at them by people who do not understand. Most frequent questions are, "Who will look after you when you are old?" and "What if everyone decided not to have kids?"'

They also provide car stickers. 'Thinker: Two Healthy Incomes, No Kids, Early Retirement' or 'No Babies on Board.'

> ANDREW: 'My wife and I are happy together. We are a loving unit. Families are in disarray and I don't want any part of it. A girl of thirteen having a baby – a woman of sixty-three having a baby, a boy of eleven a father and a man of twenty-nine a grandfather. Madness.'

The man of twenty-nine referred to had also been a father at fourteen, although he split up from his fourteen-year-old girlfriend two years after the birth of their son.

> ANDREW: 'See what I mean?'

The Millennium Family

In America the 'Millennium Woman' is now recognized. The name is given to a woman, either married or single, who remains childless as a result of deliberate choice. In the past a career woman might only have postponed having a child until her career was established. However, when a couple makes this decision jointly perhaps we see the beginning of another family grouping – The Millennium Family.

Before treatment for fertility became more successful and widespread, those couples who did not have children were in the main couples who could not have them. In the 1990s it is more likely to mean that the joint decision has been made not to become parents (Family Policy Studies Centre, October 1997).

The mistaken assumption is that every couple will want a family, although there have always been couples who have decided against parenthood. It is wise for any couple setting out together to discuss this fundamental issue concerning their marriage and life together and to leave nothing to chance.

> ALISON: *'I find the most frequent response is, "Well, I've known people who said that, and they changed their mind later."'*

Alison and her husband Jim believe there is some selective observation at work and those that do change their mind are used as ammunition against people like them.

Sally and Paul broke up after ten years of marriage:

> SALLY: *'He did say he didn't want children, but I thought he'd change his mind. Everyone wants them in time, don't they?'*

> REBECCA: *'My fiance was very supportive, once we stopped talking past each other. At first he considered it my decision, but I thought that left us open to trouble later, and so he actually then started to think about it.'*

> ROOT: *'I can't believe it when some couples talk to me. How couples have not put all their cards on the table before marriage. I say, "What do you talk about? Football?" They are victims of assumption.'*

If the relationship is strong and healthy, then a joint decision of this magnitude will be made and kept to by the couple. But it does need to be talked through. And not be a smokescreen for non-commitment.

> BELINDA: 'We made an agreement, no children. We lived together for eight years, then Ben said he was leaving me, and within a year had a child with another woman.'

With hindsight, Belinda is convinced that Ben had agreed to the 'no children' deal because he was not sure that they would be together for life.

Are child-free couples giving less to society by not having children? Strong arguments against this are that children would divert resources of time, money and energy which some couples said they wanted to use to benefit others.

> ROBERT: 'The child-free people I spoke to are concerned about things like community service, acquisition and dissemination of knowledge. I have never heard any child-free person speak of themselves. They never saw children as interfering with their planned material gains, time, etc. They avoided children in order to pursue interests and preserve the planet. I am happy with my decision.'

> SYDNEY: 'Maybe we would have had a child who would Save the World, but that would be to the credit of the child, not us.'

> BERYL: 'We will work part time. We couldn't do that if we had kids. I make my contribution by teaching, and we are happy. Doesn't the world want happy adults?'

Three out of every ten couples who divorce are childless, but there has been no research into why these marriages broke up and whether being childless was a factor. At the same time there are statistics which show the large number of couples who give very little thought to conception. Figures to support this are quoted by BON in its newsletter. One survey was carried out, of mothers who had given birth in the previous year (1989). This showed that 31 per cent of the pregnancies were unintended (Fleissig, 1991). Another survey showed that 20 per cent of conceptions end in legal abortions (*Abortion Statistics 1995* Series AB No. 22, London: Stationery Office 1997).

> BERYL: 'Just think about these figures – and people tell us we have got it wrong?'

Cohabiting v. Marriage

More couples are choosing to live together instead of marrying. Fewer than one in ten adults are in a cohabiting relationship, although this rises to one in five among younger age groups (FPS Centre, 1997). For some, this is a prelude to making the move eventually towards matrimony. For others, the way is not so clearly defined.

Cohabiting can leave some couples confused about what the commitment to each other means. We heard, 'I thought I had a partner. He thought I was a live-in girl friend.' 'I wouldn't be anyone's mistress, but I don't mind having a live-in lover.' One pitfall seems to be for couples to drift into living together. Perhaps very early on in the relationship they have sex together while still getting to know each other and then they the slip into becoming a couple.

> GRACE: *'I thought from the start we were too quick to have sex. After a couple of weeks I realized I didn't even like Tim all that much. By then he had moved in, and we kind of drifted on for the next year. I don't think either of us was happy.'*

In an article in the *Sunday Times* (8 February 1998) 'The Tender Trap', the pros and cons of cohabitation were debated. The authors had interviewed a number of couples for whom sleeping together had meant drifting into living together, and the conclusion was, 'Often the only explicit commitment in such relationships is sexual exclusivity.'

Children who have witnessed their parents' divorce may be wary about choosing marriage and having children. According to research by the Family Policy Studies Centre one of the negative effects on adult life for women who witnessed a parental divorce is that they are more likely to give birth as single or cohabiting mothers.

> MAUREEN: *'I would never trust anyone to stay for ever. I knew when I got pregnant I would be taking on total responsibility. My mother had it thrust upon her when I was three years old and my brother a new baby. This was the way I wanted it. I felt safe.'*

> CAREY: *'I haven't got over my mum and dad splitting up – there is no way I would have a baby and put myself in that position my mum found herself in after twenty years of marriage.'*

> GEORGE: *'My parents, my brother and my two sisters are divorced. How do you know if you meet the right person? I feel much safer*

living with Penny, but I suspect she may want to get married one day. I won't change my mind.'

Yet does living together with commitment but not being married, protect either partner from the pain if they break up? As we heard, Belinda thought that they would be together for always and her pain was no less severe when Ben left.

If a couple decide to cohabit, it may well mean that one of the partners is unwilling to make the commitment to marriage. All the evidence shows that cohabiting relationships last less time than married ones: two years on average (FPS Centre, 1997). However, the conclusion is that it is still 'too soon to assess the duration and stability of cohabiting relationships and whether they are replacing legal marriage'.

The political think-tank Demos is going so far as to suggest that couples should marry for a fixed term, should be able to negotiate their own vows and anyone should be able to conduct a ceremony.

At present marriage leaves a woman more financially secure in the event of a divorce or bereavement than cohabitation does. There are legal moves afoot to change the laws regarding cohabitation. The difficulty is to how to protect both partners without making the proposed registration the equivalent of marriage. Therefore, registration would most likely bring about the same reluctance to commitment in some partners. However, by registering their relationship it would mean a couple's assets could be divided by the courts if a breakup occurred. And it could provide the woman, who may well have stayed at home to look after the children, with her contribution more fairly reflected by the division of property.

Some homosexual couples do choose to live together as if married for years, and make a real and lasting commitment to each other. Nevertheless, they are not yet allowed to formalize their commitment. In other words they, unlike heterosexual couples, do not have a choice.

The Choice of Fidelity

One other choice, all too easily forgotten, was brought to our attention:

GRANT: *'Of course, most people do have a choice somewhere along the line: whether to pull themselves together and not let their marriage deteriorate to the point where divorce is inevitable.'*

Grant told us that when he is with a group of friends of his own age, he and his wife Kate are often the only couple with their original partners.

GRANT: *'We have had our difficult times, but we have also had two children together. I wouldn't be truthful if I didn't say over the years I have been attracted to other women. But – and it is this but that is important – I have chosen never to let things get out of hand.'*

KATE: *'Some friends look at us as if we are together because we haven't been tempted. Not true. We are together as a family because we believe in keeping promises.'*

The choice to stay with a partner does need to be highlighted. It is only too easy to dismiss the value of a stable relationship and simply accept that vows can be broken, as well as hearts, when a couple breaks up.

A Baby on Your Own

The testing time for a couple often comes around when one or other feels it is time to have a baby. For women, the burden is often more pressing, as they watch time go by.

CAROLINE: *'Men can hang around longer. At thirty-nine I decided to go for a baby. Alec wasn't bothered and left us a year later.'*

Caroline epitomises another category, the older, never married single mother. Some women are no longer prepared to wait – perhaps in vain – for Mr Right and feel they have the choice to have a child without the support of a partner. A woman now feels she can more easily go it alone. This has meant the proportion of women making this choice has more than doubled in the last few years, from 17 per cent to 38 per cent (Family Policy Studies Centre, October 1997). A child will be deliberately conceived either from a one-night stand or else by artificial insemination. The number of women opting for artificial insemination is on the increase: a spokesperson for the London Women's Clinic said that they are contacted by an increasing number of single heterosexual women (as well as by both heterosexual and lesbian couples). The choice has been made to have a baby, they feel, before the woman approaches the clinic. However, they do offer extensive counselling during and after treatment.

Abortion – Another Choice?

The battle cry of the pro-abortionists is, 'It's a woman's right to choose'. Those who cannot accept this idea ask what of the men? And what of the child? The situation is muddied further by telling men that the decision whether to terminate a pregnancy is 'none of their business'. And yet, if a baby is born, and the mother names the father he may well become a target for the Child Support Agency.

And what about the woman? It is not unknown for a woman who has made the choice to have a termination to feel the backlash of this for weeks, months or maybe years after the event. According to Life, an anti-abortion organization, 40 per cent of women suffer emotionally after an abortion.

> LAURA: *'I had no choice but to choose a termination. I had no partner, no family, no money, and I knew I did not have the resilience to go it alone.'*

> KAY: *'I had an abortion. I still feel sad about it and although I now have a child I keep a place in my heart for my other lost baby. Yes, we do have a choice, but I can't believe any woman today takes the decision lightly. Five years ago I had some counselling and that helped a lot. I talked and I talked, and cried and felt much less weighed down with guilt and grief afterwards.'*

> MANDY: *'I don't think of it at all. I did what I had to do. Thank God abortion is now legal. The sad thing is that my boyfriend and I broke up soon afterwards.'*

The Abortion Act (1967) does not give a woman the right to an abortion, but protects a doctor who performs one from prosecution. The choice of whether or not to continue a pregnancy is there, legally, for women. The battle rages and feelings run very high in the abortion versus pro-life camps. There have always been ways that desperate women have brought about abortions and the debate is now into the open as women are legally protected. It is the moral ground where the war is still being fought.

A constant dilemma for society as a whole should be the number of girls under the age of consent seeking contraception at Family Planning Clinics. The number has trebled in the past eight years (Office of National Statistics). Is the answer to provide condoms for children as young as thirteen? A new scheme in North Tyneside devised by health workers is designed to do just this and make condoms more accessible, saving youngsters the 'embarrassment' of having to explain themselves. There are those figures, religious and political, who oppose this project. A local Tyneside vicar feels the scheme is misguided and we should instead be teaching our children 'proper values'. The Leader of the North Tyneside Council, Michael Huscroft, holds strong, often unpopular views about the scheme.

MICHAEL HUSCROFT: *'Parents have rights and responsibilities, and these are being eroded. Youngsters should be encouraged to say "no" rather than us taking the easy option of "hand out the condoms and let them get on with it".'*

However, many of the underage girls do have intercourse without contraception and this points to the alarming statistic that eight in every 1,000 teenage girls under sixteen become pregnant. 4,000 abortions are carried out on underage girls every year. We must ask ourselves, do these children really have a choice? And what do these appalling figures say about society? The government is committed to reducing the number of pregnancies among girls under sixteen by improving sex education, but doesn't the answer lie in the example the adults should give? Again, all evidence points to the importance of a stable family background; figures show that factors in becoming a teenage parent include coming from a family with a low socio-economic status – one-parent families certainly come into this category – and experiencing emotional difficulties during childhood and adolescence.

Sadly we heard from one fifteen-year-old this comment:

SHARON: *'I went and had a baby. I wanted someone to love, and babies love you back. Don't they?'*

HAROLD: *'Children have to make choices early on. They see one or even both parents going off with another partner. Sex is shouted at us from every film, advertisement and newspaper. Just look at the tabloids on a Sunday – they are all about sex romps and adultery. No longer do we encourage and praise abstinence.'*

Single

To remain single is also a choice, and one valued by many adults. In July 1997 the Family Group of Quaker Responsibility and Education undertook an informal study on being single. Their objectives were primarily 'to promote a positive view of singleness', 'to redress the balance of emphasis on coupledom to individuality' and 'to highlight the joys and advantages of singleness'. Among the replies to their questionnaire was, 'I think it is a million times better to be single than unhappily married.'

The decision to remain single does not always mean it is the last choice.

MARIE: *'My parents split up when I was five, and my marriage ended after three years. I am now on my own and feel content and happy.'*

ANTHONY: *'Well, I can't call myself a family. I am an independent unit. I wish it had been otherwise, but there it is.'*

MAXINE: *'I am single, but I most certainly am part of a large extended family.'*

From others we heard once more of prejudice: 'People see single as odd' and 'No one believes I am content to be celibate.' Yet this was rejected by those with a more optimistic view who felt that being single brought with it new opportunities and was a positive choice.

Proceed with Caution

The choices we have considered are wide and disparate and each in its own way has its gains and losses. While the diversity brings about freedom of choice for many, it prompts disapproval from others, since most of us feel comfortable with people who are similar and resent variations from familiar patterns. Whichever path we select, ultimately we will have to bear the responsibility for selecting that option. These are decisions which will affect us for the rest of our lives, so they should be embarked on only after long and careful consideration.

10 The Family Today and Tomorrow

I give you this pledge. Every area of this Government's policy will be scrutinised to see how it affects family life. Every policy examined, every initiative tested, to see how we strengthen our families.

Prime Minister Tony Blair *30 December 1997*

The Changing Pattern

The changes in the pattern of family life over the last fifty years have been on a massive scale and very rapid. Each one of us is affected in some way by the proliferation in the number of divorces, and by the variations in the structure of families. More and more children are born outside of marriage: in Britain as many as one in three (statistics from Family Policy Studies Centre). Figures show a rise in the number of couples cohabiting before marriage and also after divorce. One-parent families and stepfamilies are ever on the increase. What do all these changes mean to the children involved?

Half a century ago John Bowlby warned of the risk to society if we ignored the fact that, 'mother love in infancy is as important for mental health as are vitamins and proteins for physical health' (Bowlby, 1953). From different disciplines has come the evidence that babies need a constant loving carer and a stable environment, without which the child will later experience, among many other things, anxiety and loss of self-esteem as an adult. Earlier we looked at the way that D.W. Winnicott spoke of the importance of the *father* supporting the *mother* to look after the *children*. More and more research shows that children suffer when their family falls apart. In March 1996 Professor Richard Whitfield gave a paper 'The Economic and Social Costs of Family Disintegration' in Rome (at the conference on The Family and Economy in the Future of Society) warning once more of the dire effects of family breakdown. He reminded us that the impact of the Second World War is still embedded in family psychological history because of the insecurities and bereavements involved. He insists that family breakdown is not a brief occurrence, but generally has lifelong implications. 'Family breakdown is akin in most cases to a social and psychological "holocaust".' Why have we not listened to these, and other, repeated warnings? When the family unit is shattered, the pieces have to be put back together, but in what order? Will they ever come together again in a satisfactory way?

Sheila Switzer, who coordinates the Cambridge Bowlby Group, spoke to us of her despair at getting across the message that young children do need consistent, loving care. The childcare issue is where the feminist approach founders. Women struggling for opportunities to gain ground in the workforce have somehow lost sight of the importance of being a mother. Not so Alison Holley, who gave up her opportunity to be a parliamentary candidate. As the mother of three children aged ten, five and two, she realized she already had a full-time job, and 'one that is best served by my actual presence full time at home'. Alison would have dearly liked to have become a 'voice' in Parliament, and feels that the women already elected have by the very nature of things chosen differently.

ALISON HOLLEY: *'Who is going to defend the rights of the full-time mother and represent the view that this is a vital, fulfilling and important role for both mother and child, as well as for society? The change will have to come from the men.'*

What is also being lost is the belief that children need nurturing; we are in danger of forgetting that the children of today are our investment in the future. But, it is not fashionable to labour this point, and many men and women who are in a position to voice these grave concerns are silent. Some home-caring parents believe society sees them as indulging in a personal hobby; it is often not politically correct to say publicly that the best person to look after a baby or young child is its mother.

The Child Poverty Action Group, a charity dedicated to the relief of poverty among children and families with children, *has* led the way by calling on the government to give *real* choices to lone parents. The report, in 1998, draws together all the evidence concerning the problems faced by lone parents who have to bring up their children on low incomes. It also challenges the myths and prejudices adopted towards single parents, and explores what needs to be done to enable parents to exercise responsible choices on behalf of their children. They delivered a manifesto to 10 Downing Street in March 1998 which has the support of many groups including Barnardo's, the Children's Society, the National Council for One Parent Families, Gingerbread and the Single Parent Action Network. The information officer for the Child Poverty Action Group told us that she was disappointed, but not surprised, that the press gave little coverage to the report. Sadly, the facts, while solid were not new and therefore not seen as 'news'. However, the launch of the report was held at the House of Commons and did draw attention to the message.

The Children's Society has launched a campaign to develop innovative ways to find and protect children who run away from home or from Care each year. These are young children who have fallen through the safety net of their families.

In Exeter, there is a small group of professionals led by a GP, Dr Adrian Rogers. They call themselves the Conservative Family Institute and are not afraid to speak out in favour of supporting the traditional family. Dr Rogers feels passionately about family issues and bemoans the fact that there is no interest in investing public funding for research into conventional families. Meanwhile his small group do all they can to provide information and to underline the value and worth of the traditional family. Dr Rogers believes we are all guilty of neglecting the gravity of the situation by ignoring the distress caused by the growing numbers of broken families.

Anyone speaking out for mothers who stay at home to look after their children is at risk of being accused of wanting to turn the clock back and to make *all* women once more spend all their time in the kitchen. Mothers, whether single or married, are under financial pressure to return to work and the emphasis on paid employment takes no account of the labour involved by mothers caring for their infants. Inevitably women who have struggled to gain equal work opportunities with men face a dilemma about whether or not to acknowledge that young children need their mothers at home to care for them. Too often the cry is 'we can have it all', but we cannot. For some women, it seems to be a badge of honour to return to work within days of having given birth to a baby. Yet, as Dr Peter Cook's worldwide coverage of research into infant care shows, poor quality day care will interfere with the child's intellectual and emotional development. Universal, affordable good quality childcare is unrealistic in today's world.

Ten years ago Valerie Grove in *The Complete Woman* (1987) interviewed twenty working mothers – all high flyers – and one conclusion she reached was, 'Feminism and family life are hard to reconcile, but reconciled they have to be.' She also observed that the 'complete woman' needs a man, and all these women had strong marriages. She was critical of Dr John Bowlby and felt he laid too much guilt upon the mothers who wanted or needed to work. Although with those mothers who could afford to pay for help with the children she noted, 'No woman who lets another woman look after her children while she herself is busy working can ever be entirely free

from the nagging expectation of a later reproach from the children.'
The fathers, she pointed out, were never blamed. 'It was the mother,
who when the children were older had to cover the 4–6.30 slot.' How
the wheels have turned, and how much harder, ten years later, to be a
mother, single or married in a low income family, and have to arrange
affordable childcare. BBC Panorama, in its programme 'Childcare on
the Cheap' (March 1998), showed a shocking view of much nursery
care. Two young mothers had managed to find work and a place for
their children in a nursery. After seeing the secret recordings of what
had taken place, they had no choice but to withdraw their babies and
give up their jobs. How very hard it must have been for the countless
other mothers watching this programme to view the truly abusive and
neglectful care of young children and yet have no option if they work.
The nursery 'carers' seemed to be, on the whole, young inexperienced
girls who were very poorly paid, with minimal training or supervision
in childcare.

Why Get Married?

Today, both parents are felt to be, at least in part, responsible for the
child when there is a breakup of the family, and fathers as well as
mothers feel anguish at seeing headlines such as 'Broken homes, the
breeding ground for young criminals' (*Daily Mail*, March 1998). Sadly,
in this report, young children who are at risk of becoming criminals
were, as usual, linked with 'parental neglect' and 'the breakup of the
traditional two-parent family'; thus once again imprinting on people's
minds that *all* single-parent families are problem families.

In earlier chapters we saw the ways that families come together in
different constellations and how new family groupings bring about
new challenges, and also fresh solutions. Couples who want to remain
childless, whether they marry or not, are at liberty to choose their
lifestyle and to take advantage of the lessening of the stigma of earlier
years when cohabiting was synonymous with 'living in sin'. And
where there are no children, and the relationship breaks down, the
man or woman is free to develop an independent and separate life.

For those who do choose to marry, the figures show disconcerting
odds against them celebrating a golden wedding. With such alarming
statistics about the failure of marriage why then do couples still go
through with it? The consensus of opinion from the men and women
who spoke to us is that couples still get married because they want to
make a public declaration of their love and trust in each other. Also,
that 'tradition' continues to be valued, and there are still couples who

want to make their vows to each other before God. The Church does teach that marriage is for life. However the Church is seen by many to be in the process of being swayed by the changes in society and its view on endorsing divorce and remarriage is one area where there is little clarity. Religious belief is often a personal marker that acknowledges the welfare of others, not only of oneself. This would seem to be a good foundation for a lasting marriage and for rearing children. Marriage involves more than just a promise to stay together 'in sickness and in health'. It is an affirmation of total trust.

In Chapter 2 we heard Elizabeth Longford's views on relationships. She holds equally firm views about marriage.

ELIZABETH LONGFORD: 'The specialness of marriage from a human and religious point of view has to be appreciated. Otherwise, why are you giving up all the experiences available outside – the chance of other relationships? What have you got instead? The Church does not emphasize enough the positive side of marriage.'

Terry Waite, whose absence for five years during his incarceration as a hostage in Beirut put a tremendous strain on his wife and family, has strong views on the family and divorce.

TERRY WAITE: 'If society slackens its boundaries – and it has – and if divorce becomes too easy, couples will break up at the first hurdle. The children are always the ones who get hurt the most.'

So often the quest for personal fulfilment is sought at the expense of the children's right to happiness. If two adults have a child, as parents they are responsible for the welfare of that child whatever happens to their own personal relationship. In The Politics of Hope (1997) Chief Rabbi Dr Jonathan Sacks puts the point firmly on the behalf of the children of broken marriages:

Chief Rabbi Dr JONATHAN SACKS: 'A single breakdown of order introduces into our horizons a note of mistrust and we are never free again. Betrayed once as partners or children, we are reluctant to give ourselves wholly and unconditionally to another person.'

The family is the basic unit of society and we have seen how some adults and children struggle together to mend this safety net when it is breaking under the strain of external or internal pressures. If the family unit breaks down everyone is at sea:

BOB: *'No one told me how to be a divorced parent.'*

No one tells children, either, how to be a child of divorce. There is still a lack of guidelines about how to manage the collapse of a family, especially in relation to the children. Trial and error are painful.

All the evidence shows that children of divorce do get hurt. The ways children are affected both in the short and long term are numerous. This cannot be repeated too often. Children need a safe, loving atmosphere in which to grow into happy, well-adjusted adults, and in time to be parents to their own children. As we have seen, research has shown that those who experience the divorce of their parents during childhood are more likely to see their own partnership or marriage break up than those whose parents stay together. In other words, divorce breeds divorce.

The Slow Way Forward

We have seen how after a divorce the 'new' families – of which 90 per cent are made up of lone mothers – struggle to keep their heads above water, both financially and emotionally. We have seen how the lone parent is most likely to be an older woman, and divorced, separated or widowed. Hopefully the myth has been dispelled that all lone mothers are young and 'feckless', relish living on benefit and are workshy. In fact the young, uneducated and unemployed single mother accounts for only 3.7 per cent of all lone mothers (Child Poverty Action Group Report).

If a parent remarries and a stepfamily is created this is a delicate time for each member of the family. For the parent remarrying there is often a conflict of interests in having to look in two directions at the same time. For the adult marrying for the first time there is the difficulty of building a new married life with the shadow of the old making itself felt. The child has to swallow the bitter pill that the parents will not get back together again. However stormy the relationship has been many children nurse a secret hope this will be so.

As we saw in Chapter 3 careful preparations have to be made if the new relationship is to get off to a good start. Children have to be kept informed and allowances made for them, particularly if the child has to go backwards and forwards between two families. Frequently conflicts of loyalty arise; it must never be forgotten that it is difficult for a child to live with one parent and 'visit' the other, perhaps more so if a new baby arrives.

ANDREW, who was six when his parents divorced, and seven when his father remarried: *'Being in a stepfamily? I didn't ever get over all the changes. I just got used to them.'*

The stepfamilies who found the transition less stressful than others were the families who found ways of developing a new family history encompassing all the members, asked for help when it was needed and perhaps, above all, where the parents gave time to developing a relationship with each child before attempting to discipline them. Stepfamilies do represent a new investment in the future, and for the partner who marries someone who already has children there are different pitfalls to be wary of, whether the child is two or twenty-two. But love can move mountains, and goes a long way towards making a new family – especially when the new parents recognize that the path is hard for the children who may still be grieving over the loss of their original family.

CHERYL WALTERS: *'All the family members need the opportunity to spend time alone together. The couple, stepparent and stepchild, parent with child, even parent with stepparent, even as little as ten minutes give the chance to be in touch with important things that matter.'*

Therefore, by trying to go at a pace to suit everybody and being aware of the hazards, the stepfamily is on its way. Keep in mind that the National Stepfamily Association believes it takes between two and ten years for a stepfamily to settle.

Who Can I Turn To?

More divorced parents means more children being cared for by lone parents, so who steps in if there is another crisis in the family? This is the time when grandparents can sometimes be on hand to offer support for the single-parent family. But this is not as straightforward as it may seem, and the number of grandparents who are forbidden any contact with their grandchildren causes concern. A recent fight in court between a grandmother and the lesbian ex-lover of the child's mother over the child's custody was lost by the grandmother. This was after the intervention of the Official Solicitor, Peter Harris, who is the Senior Legal Guardian of Children's Welfare in England and Wales. This was a complicated situation, and it is the first case of a lesbian winning legal custody of an unrelated child against a family member. Previously, lesbian and gay men have won custody of an unrelated child *only* when a child has been removed from the extended family after they were unable to cope. The grandmother had been fighting for custody for six years. Three years ago the natural mother left the child in the care of her ex-partner, so to all intents and purposes the woman who was awarded custody had been mother to the child for several years.

As we saw in Chapter 6 there are a growing number of grandparents who take on the role of parenting – not grandparenting – but parenting their grandchildren. Not all grandparents welcome this new obligation. While many took on this task with love, they also had to struggle with their resentment, and the anxiety that this situation had come about in the first place. The grandparents who make up the Peterborough Group found the main cause which brought about the collapse of their families had been their children's choice of an unsuitable partner. The daily grind was a physical struggle and if there were gains there were also losses. As we heard from Linda, after caring for her grandchild she felt she lost the privilege and joy of 'just being a granny'. And from another grandma:

> SUZANNE: *'I have six other grandchildren. But, sadly, no time for them. That is a huge loss both to my husband and myself, and for my grandchildren who have grandparents so busy bringing up their two cousins that I can't be a gran to them at all. I feel the grief of that. But what could we do?'*

Indeed, what could they do? This was asked again and again as the older generation tried to put right some of the mistakes made by their children in order to provide a stable family life for the grandchildren. Two of the most frequent comments were, 'Faith in God helped us through', and 'My prayers were answered, I had the strength to go on.'

> ALICE: *'I know what it is like. My father was away in the war for years. I didn't really ever get to know him. When he came home we probably looked like a family from the outside, but we weren't in the home. I left home at sixteen and got married, and that went wrong a few years later. I felt really bad about bringing up a child without a father, even though the reason was different. Now my daughter's marriage is in collapse, I care for my little granddaughter and try to give her a home, but its not right. A child needs a mum and a dad. I should know.'*

Parenting a second time around was always done with love, but often with a very heavy heart.

Gay and Lesbian Family Groups

In Britain the government is paving the way to accept same-sex partners by offering the same privileges and rights to the partners of all MPs. For immigration purposes there is now a growing recognition of same-sex relationships. And yet there is still widespread prejudice. A lesbian couple's claim for the same rights as heterosexuals to the perks of a partner's job was thrown out by the European Court in February 1998. The Court agreed that discrimination based on *sex* was illegal but that discrimination based on *sexual orientation* was not yet illegal under European law. The fight will continue, leading to a stronger call to legalize same-sex marriages. As so often the balance is delicate, trying to wipe out discrimination while at the same time ensuring that matrimony retains its special status and that the family as we know it is safeguarded.

Prejudice, albeit disguised, often arises unexpectedly. Thelma Gabriel runs a helpline for parents who are bewildered to hear that their sons or daughters are homosexual. She spoke with us and said that the helpline Parents Together arose out of her own family situation. She said the shock of being told by her son that he is gay left her 'like a zombie' at first. She imagined the gossip which would follow the disclosure – 'They seemed a nice family' – until she realized it was her *own* prejudice speaking. A recent article in a woman's magazine brought forth a flood of telephone calls to her helpline, with the comment from one grief-stricken mother, 'I didn't know there was *anybody* I could talk to.'

Nowhere is prejudice more evident than in relation to a homosexual couple with a child. It may have become easier to be 'out' as a lesbian or gay, but there is still some considerable way to go before there is wider acceptance of sexual orientation in cases where a child is involved. Most same-sex couples with a child are a result of a previous heterosexual relationship by one of the partners, although some couples do opt for insemination. A landmark decision was made in 1997 when an eleven-year-old girl was placed for adoption with a couple, both of whom are lesbian. Until then, as the law stood, if a couple were both homosexual only one, not both, could make an application for adoption. Equally strong reactions are found when fostering a child is debated. There is nothing in the Children Act, which regulates fostering, to suggest that lesbians and gay men should not foster children, but in practice it is sometimes difficult for lesbians and gay men to become foster carers as some agencies and some local authorities still practice discrimination. The National Foster Care Association and the Lesbian and Gay Fostering and Adoptive Parents' Network have collaborated to produce an information pack which is full of helpful advice, and details of agencies sympathetic to the situation. It also challenges the myth that men cannot bring up children without women, and reinforces the view that the most important role model for a child is one of a loving, caring human being.

As we heard from Bonnie and Susie in Chapter 5, it is not easy to become a co-parent to a partner's child and a gay family face, on top of everything else, many of the divided loyalties and jealousies encountered by the stepfamily. Speaking with gay couples left us in no doubt of the love for their children which many of them have, and of the anxieties that many of them feel because their non-traditional family group is on the receiving end of prejudiced opinion. It is to be hoped that the stereotyped thinking aimed at a child living with a same-sex couple has been challenged.

The Future of the Family

This government is committed to supporting families, and the 1998 Budget confirmed this. Chancellor Gordon Brown (March 1998) spoke of families as 'the bedrock of a stable and healthy society' and guaranteed financial help for childcare. He raised child benefit for the eldest child and gave advantageous tax allowances for low-paid working families. Critics of this feel that the tax credit for childcare will be an incentive for some lone mothers to leave their children, who are already coping with the loss of one parent, to be minded. Another criticism is that there is a serious shortage of qualified playworkers and childminders. Anne Longfield, director of Kids' Club Network says more staff will have to be trained, and supervision and quality control must be in place. She believes a whole new profession is needed to cope with the proposed increase of 30,000 clubs.

> ANNE LONGFIELD: 'We are going to need about 90,000 new playworkers to staff the extra kids' clubs, and there simply aren't the facilities there to train them all quickly enough at present.'

The choice of a partner has lasting impact, not only today but on future generations. And it is to them our collective responsibilities lie.

If we do not take seriously obligations towards others and if we do not value commitments made, how can we provide standards for our children? In America a new idea is a 'love contract' for employees to sign if they become involved with a colleague at work. It shows they have agreed to a mutually consenting amorous relationship. The contract has been devised to protect the companies and the individuals involved if the relationship comes to grief. Where is the trust in this?

Chief Rabbi Dr Jonathan Sacks explains the difference between a 'contract' and a 'covenant'. A covenant brings with it a moral obligation and a response to someone else beyond the letter of the law. A contract can be broken, but a covenant binds two people, maybe more so in difficult times. 'This is because a covenant is not predicated on interest, but instead on loyalty, fidelity, holding together even when things seem to be driving you apart' (Sacks, 1997). These are considerations which are totally ignored when thinking of a 'love contract', when the focus is on financial protection or claims of sexual harassment, with no regard for the quality of the relationship.

On one hand we hear from those who are speaking about the decline of the family and of the neglected children in the modern family maze. On the other there are men and women who say they accept welcome changes to the family structure. Today's climate encourages people to speak out, and to try to do something about their position. Everything is possible; perhaps by making fresh choices and fresh starts there is more honesty and sincerity about facing up to intolerable situations:

TREVOR HARTNUP, Chair of the Association of Child Psychotherapists: *'There have always been happy and unhappy families. There has always been stress in some families, sexual acting out, and aggression. That is not new. What is new is that this is all much more unregulated because it is not tempered by secure attachments or supported by a wider accepted social structure. Different family combinations are more difficult to maintain if there are no guidelines. If there are no solid social expectations, it forces young people to find something else – and this may be drugs or alcohol.'*

What do we want from a family? Looking at the extremely high viewing figures for nightly 'soaps' suggests there is great interest in family life, even if it is only representative of dysfunctional television families. There is a fascination about the way relationships unfold on our screens. The irony is that the families sitting with their supper on trays in front of the television, watching the family dramas unfold, often neglect their own household. It is easier to deal with the tragicomedy of a family at arm's length, than to be involved with the sorrows and pleasures which make up real life.

At the end of the day, it is not how a family is labelled, 'traditional', 'step', 'gay', 'child-free' or 'one-parent', but what the interaction is like between the members of the family: whether or not they look after each other, whether there are people to turn to, to huddle with if the outside world is cold. Are we able to see each family for what it is, without being blinded by preconceptions and a view which is a stereotype and a way of placing people in a pigeonhole?

Those who despair about the future of the family should consider these facts provided by the Family Policy Studies Centre.

- Four out of five families are headed by a couple.

- The definition of a family still includes more than one generation.

- Research shows that the family is still the main source of care for the old and disabled.

- As the family changes, the policy makers are studying how to arrange a partnership of care between the statutory and voluntary sectors together with family carers. It is estimated that there are 6.8 million carers in Britain – the majority of whom are caring for another family member.

- Family members still live close to each other – two-thirds of adult children live within an hour's journey time of their mothers. And 76 per cent of people see the family as more important than friends.

Remember, too, the couples who spoke with us after thirty, forty or more years of marriage. They do not, on the whole, make the headlines and we are more likely to read of serial relationships, abandoned 'exes' and disturbed children, than those who have spent almost a lifetime together.

Among the newspapers the *Daily Mail* and *The Times* adopt a pro-family stance. Simon Jenkins wrote a leader in *The Times* (11 April 1998) about the plight of desperate parents and families. Believing as he does that 'family life is bruising' he is amazed that most children manage to survive at all. Parents weighed down by unemployment and poor housing 'take it out on each other and their children'. If the situation becomes too harsh 'they relieve its pressure by divorce'. Outside support for struggling parents is needed. For the more affluent, nannies or even boarding school are a 'respite from the strain of parenthood'. He finds it remarkable 'that most children whose development surely demands an extended society, contrive to survive nuclear families at all'. He is saddened by the fact that there are parents who may love their children, but 'who foul it up'. No amount of preaching about family values can help parents sinking under the weight of a hopeless situation.

Hillary Rodham Clinton, the US President's wife, chose the title of her book *It Takes a Village* (1996) from an old African proverb because, 'It offers a timeless reminder that children will thrive only if their families thrive and if the whole of society cares enough to provide for them.' And do we? Supporting the family means many things, and decent housing, secure employment and effective education would go a long way to do just that.

Perhaps a hopeful sign of support of another kind is the announcement that the government is beginning to live up to its promises to care for the family. A proposal is afoot to provide fathers with a statutory minimum paternity payment, partly funded by the state, of one week's paternity leave. In the pipeline are plans to provide three months' unpaid parental leave for all working parents, both mothers and fathers. Unpaid parental leave will be introduced in December 1999 when Britain adopts the European Commission's Social Chapter. These proposals could reinforce the importance of the father to be more accessible when a baby is born and more able to take an active role in caring for the infant – a good beginning for any family.

Not only from my research for this book, but from my own experience first as a social worker for many years with a hands-on job with families, and then as a psychoanalytic psychotherapist, I have spoken to countless men, women and children about their experiences of family life. I have seen the way people will struggle in therapy to understand and to untangle difficulties within themselves in order to protect or safeguard loved ones. Often the spur to seek professional help has been the desire to break the chain of painful family experiences. I have seen how many people struggle against all odds to preserve their family and to gather around them those they love. In previous chapters we have heard from numerous men and women all doing their best to keep a family together. Of course some families collapse under the strain, usually from either financial worries or emotional stress, and we must praise the courage of those who despite these burdens rally to care for the children, the innocent casualties of the broken family. We depend on each other, and interdependence is essential to create and sustain families. It is vital we appreciate the need to connect with others as well as the ability to be separate. The chemistry of each family is different and develops its own way of forging strong links between its members while each of them also conserves an individual identity. We must also cherish the caring quality of the family – care of the elderly, of the disabled, of the children, and of each other. The picture is not entirely bleak. In this book we have observed the breakup of many families, but we have also looked at the remaking of families and seen how many couples carry this through successfully.

It is comforting to learn from Wallerstein's studies of children of divorce that there are ways children can be helped through this time: firstly, if the divorce is undertaken thoughtfully by parents who have carefully considered the alternatives, and they have taken on board the severe consequences for themselves and the children; secondly, they have taken every possible step to safeguard the children, and made it possible for them to maintain a good parent–child relationship with both parents. If so, then 'children are not likely to suffer developmental interference or enduring psychological distress as a consequence'. What can harm children is the disrupted parenting which so often follows in the wake of the breakup and 'which can become consolidated within the post-divorce family'. Even though the children may still regret that their parents can no longer love each other 'some of these children may nevertheless grow in their capacity for compassion and psychological understanding'.

In June 1998, *The Times* carried a report ('Hopes and Fears: Young European Opinion Leaders') that three thousand teenagers had been interviewed by a British research team, GfK, to find out what today's youth want for tomorrow. Most of the teenagers were children of broken homes. Their unanimous answer was 'a happy family'. There was universal condemnation of divorce, demands that parents should keep their vows, and admiration for stable couples.

Warm, loving families can be created from the devastation of a broken family only if all the adults combine to protect the children and do not minimize the impact on them as they struggle to cope with the changes in the adult world. We have not heard from the majority of families, those who just get on with the day-to-day job of living together and making a family strong.

The family may not be as recognizable as it once was, but it still thrives in a variety of ways. As well as the old, there are new patterns, and we must learn to recognize them and to support and to value them.

Chief Rabbi Dr JONATHAN SACKS: *'The family will prove to be the axis on which our moral world will turn.'*

11 Professional Support

For addresses and other detailed information
see Chapter 12 'Resources'

Both in the making and the breaking of families there are times when
help may be needed, sometimes on a practical matter, for example
legal rights, and frequently on an emotional level. The difficulty is
where to get the right support at the right time. When a marriage is in
crisis one of the first experts to be consulted is often a solicitor. This
can be a drastic step to take, a serious procedure which often brings
with it the realization that the marriage has finally reached breaking
point. Using professional legal advisers can often be very costly and all
too frequently one hears the comment, 'Nobody wins except the
solicitors.'

LEGAL HELP

The Solicitors Family Law Association

In 1982 the Solicitors Family Law Association was formed because
some solicitors were concerned that legal wrangling too often added to
distress at the time of the breakdown of a relationship. The association believes that solutions must be found which do not destroy the
possibility of family members continuing to deal with each other in a
civilized way. This is, of course, especially important when it is
necessary to reach agreement over the children. The association also
accepts that 'agreed solutions are more likely to be adhered to and
prove durable than those imposed by a court'. Perhaps more importantly they feel that with less bitterness aroused 'the greater the
chance of forming secure new relationships and raising well-adjusted
children'. A leaflet giving ten good reasons why there is an advantage
to choose a member of the Solicitors Family Law Association is
available, and they have produced *A Guide to Good Practice for
Solicitors Acting for Children*. The Law Society recommends that all
solicitors practising family law should follow the code of practice of the
SFLA.

The Family Law Act 1996

New Labour is committed to supporting marriages and has endorsed the changes in the divorce law of the Family Law Act 1996 due to be implemented in 1999. Anyone working with families should be aware of the adjustment in thinking that this will bring about.

Accepting that some couples who expected marriage to be for life may reach a point when they feel they can no longer continue in the relationship, the government's objective is to establish laws which 'enable couples to consider fully whether they really want a divorce before it is granted'. They want to ensure that all couples have full information on the options available *before* deciding to divorce.

Couples wanting to start divorce proceedings will be obliged to attend an Information Meeting, either jointly or separately. In this way, it is hoped that marriages that can be saved will be identified. Either way, it will ensure couples have the necessary time and information needed to consider making this momentous decision.

The guiding principle will be that the institution of marriage should be supported, and couples will be encouraged to take every practical step possible and to have counselling in order to save the marriage. The Information Meeting will be exactly what it sounds like: information about where to go for advice will be given – this should not be confused with mediation; and leaflets about services and agencies which can provide further assistance will be distributed.

The heart of the new process will be a 'passage for the period for reflection and consideration', a period for the couple to consider the full implications and to agree on arrangements for the children, and on finance. This will last for a period of a minimum of nine months, and a further six months where there are children in the family who are under sixteen years of age.

The Family Law Act is a truly radical reform. No longer will the emphasis be on the past history of the couple's relationship. The aim of the reform is to encourage the parties to look forward, and to take responsibility for their future. Irretrievable breakdown of marriage will remain the sole ground for divorce, and divorce will only be granted after the completion of due legal process.

The Law Commission urged the introduction of a 'good' divorce law which should support and not undermine the institution of marriage. Where divorce is inevitable, the process should protect the couple *and* the children from additional stress. If the marriage is being brought to an end it should be 'with minimum distress to the parties and children affected'.

Hearing in the previous chapters from men and women – and children – involved in divorce makes one all too aware of the distress and turmoil for those who were not given the benefit of advice and counselling. They experienced a great loss in not being able to take advantage of the new understanding in the 'ways in which children can be helped to cope with the breakdown of a marriage'.

There are more legal changes afoot. The Lord Chancellor has revealed a new proposal (March 1998) for unmarried fathers to be given the same rights and parental responsibilities as married men. But if a consultation paper on these lines does go forward will it further undermine marriage by removing the bias against unmarried fathers? Under existing law the unmarried father has no such rights or responsibilities unless both parents sign an agreement that is witnessed and registered in court. Not surprisingly, not many couples know about this. Families Need Fathers, who are more concerned with the fathers' rights than with the sanctity of marriage, feel this is a change long overdue: these proposals would enhance a father's role and many fathers would be willing to take on these obligations. The current laws discriminate against a father who wants to be seen as a responsible parent though not married to the mother of his child.

WHO TO TALK TO?

When a family is in crisis, it can be very difficult to decide who to turn to for advice and help in managing the emotional storm which rages. Members of an extended family are often the first ports of call where they are available. But because of a difficult family history this possibility may not be quite as straightforward or as helpful as it originally seems. Special friends? Most women do talk to a friend, although it seems harder for a man to do this. And from women we heard of their anxiety in confiding very personal details at a time of crisis, with fear of gossip and maybe betrayal of a confidence later.

There *are* people to talk to, in fact an army of people is willing and able to give support on almost any situation, but research and effort are often needed to seek them out. Time and again, in different situations, people told us 'I didn't think there was anybody else in this situation', 'I really did not think that anybody could help me', 'How on earth do you begin to find someone else in the same boat?' and 'I felt so alone.'

Counselling and Psychotherapy

There are sometimes anxieties about turning to a professional for help with a family problem. No one who works in the counselling or psycho-therapy professions ever loses sight of the courage it takes for someone to pick up the telephone to ask for an appointment. Counselling is a much overused word, although acknowledgement and recognition of counsel-ling as a profession is growing. For someone who has trained and quali-fied through a respected organization is it galling to hear the word used as indiscriminately as it is. There are major differences between talking to a volunteer, however sympathetic, a volunteer trained by a specific organi-zation to deal with a specific issue, and a trained and qualified counsellor who will provide support during a crisis in a person's life. If the proper help is available at the right time, it can prevent the development of a deeper problem later. Indeed, it is possible to prevent the formation of a full-blown crisis. If short-term counselling is offered, it may well mean the counsellor is more directive and the work more in contact with the current circumstances.

There has been a huge surge in the number of different organizations offering training both in counselling and psychotherapy. The training for both these professions is now more regulated, and directories listing members who have been trained to a high professional standard are available from the British Association for Counselling, the British Confederation of Psychotherapists and the United Kingdom Council for Psychotherapy.

Some people who want to increase their understanding of them-selves may not expect a quick solution and are prepared to work towards a fundamental change over a long period. How do you know if counselling or psychotherapy would be the best way forward? One way is to approach an organization such as the British Association of Psychotherapists for an assessment to see whether individual psycho-therapy would be helpful.

What happens in an assessment? Some of the assessors for the Clinical Service of the British Association of Psychotherapists have contributed essays to *Assessment in Psychotherapy* (Cooper and Alfillé 1998) and these experiences of psychotherapists demonstrate the effectiveness and purpose of a consultation with a skilled practitioner.

As any counsellor in any setting soon discovers, both couples and individuals are often disappointed not to be given an immediate solu-tion. They have a problem, and if they have the courage to seek out a professional they expect to find an answer. This is, of course, to see the problem primarily as an external one and to ignore the conflict which has built up inside. When a relationship breaks down, and someone looks for help, the familiar cry of 'Why has this happened to me?' is heard by counsellors and psychotherapists. Another hope is that 'the professional' will place the blame squarely on the other's shoulders. Child psychotherapist Trevor Hartnup has found that families always expect child psychotherapists to take away the children's pain, and they may not be able to do so.

If concerned about the relationship of a couple, then the Tavistock Marital Studies Institute may well be the place to contact. Their psychoanalytic approach looks at the unconscious interaction and earlier blueprints held by both of the partners. The relationship between the couple (and the therapist) and how they came to choose each other will be considered, and also the way they see each other and the outside world, together with their fears and fantasies. But it is not always easy for a couple to accept this exploration of their internal worlds. Although it may be 'good to talk' it may not be an easy thing to do. As an assessor for many years for the Clinical Service of the British Association of Psychotherapists I was always very conscious of just how difficult it was for most people to arrive in a stranger's consulting room and say 'I need some help' and immediately to reveal very personal details about themselves and their life.

Telephone Helplines

Telephone helplines are coordinated, on the whole, by men and women who give their time to help others going through a crisis they have themselves faced, and this is perhaps one of the reasons why they are so valued. These concerned people are dedicated to listening, and to passing on their own understanding and empathy about a particular situation. Helplines for specific problems have been referred to throughout this book. The combined help these volunteers give should never be underestimated or undervalued. These helplines are very effective in supplying information about local support and resources. Very often we were told, 'I had no one to turn to', 'I couldn't tell anybody, and then I saw the helpline telephone number', 'They were there for me when no one else was', and perhaps the most telling of all, 'They listened and gave me all the time I needed.'

The Samaritans

When considering the value of telephone support the Samaritans immediately come to mind. They received 4.2 million calls in the

United Kingdom and the Republic of Ireland in the year 1996. That was a 9 per cent increase over the previous year. They do not pigeonhole their callers, so there is no record of the reason why someone calls. The Information Officer told us that the focus for help is on 'feelings, not facts'.

Childline

The telephone no longer holds the trepidation it did for earlier generations, and the number for Childline, which is twelve years old this year, is available to most school children. Children do have worries, and, according to Childline, the most common causes for a call are bullying and the unhappiness about a relationship at home. The number of children in distress is staggering, and Childline reports that although they receive 3,000 calls a day, to be answered by their trained volunteers, there are far more calls than they can answer. Children often do feel safer confiding in an unknown, unseen telephone counsellor than face to face with someone they know.

More than four million callers to the Samaritans and three thousand calls a day to Childline – what does this reveal about the unhappiness of many people today? Why do we need volunteers to listen to our children, our colleagues, our neighbours and, of course, members of our family? Is it that we are 'too busy' to listen, or that we do not want to know about the misery which exists?

Carers National Association

There are more than 6.8 million carers in the UK involved in the day-to-day care of a relative or friend providing largely unseen family support (General Household Survey, 1990). Families who look after elderly and disabled relatives at home are to get a 'care charter' setting out their rights. This help is designed to encourage families to look after the elderly at home. The new charter will be implemented before the Royal Commission on Care of the Elderly reports at the end of 1998.

More recently the value of these dedicated men and women has been recognized; carers themselves can feel isolated and they in turn need support; so the Carers National Association now has information about support groups and services available to help the carers.

GPs

When people are in trouble one of the most likely places to go is their GP's surgery. Stress about a personal relationship can often be hidden both from the patient and the doctor by a cluster of physical symptoms. While some general practitioners may resent this further burden on their time, others are more aware of the difficulties being experienced and will spend extra time with a patient helping him or her to explore what the underlying cause of an illness may be.

Moreover, with a growing number of counsellors attached to practices there is more help available for many patients. Family doctors are discovering that the appointment of a counsellor means containing more patients within the practice, and there are fewer referrals to outside consultants. Asking for help with an emotional or psychological problem is still felt by some to be an admission of not coping, and for this reason many prefer to approach a professional with a practical problem, but in this way people who would not have had access to a counsellor find themselves referred for help.

While some counsellors will bring a psychodynamic understanding to their work, others will approach the problem from a systemic point of view and are trained to work with the family. According to Dr Curtis-Jenkins, the Director of the Primary Health Care Trust, 'Everything depends on the capacity of the therapist to create empathy and an alliance – the most important areas related to change.' The question of whether counselling in a medical setting is cost-effective is one of the areas considered in *Psychotherapy and Counselling in Primary Health Care* by Wiener and Sher (1998). These authors give case examples, to demonstrate their thinking, of the kind of help offered to individuals who are referred for help, and also to families who are often heavy users of the surgery's services. They believe that:

> *A psychodynamic approach to counselling in primary care should go hand in hand with a psychodynamic understanding of health care systems, the stresses they generate and the way they are costed. It is not possible to understand and address the issue of cost in any system that operated in ignorance of unconscious processes at work.*

There is support for professionals working in this area, and the Thinking Families Network (TFN) provides a supportive educational network for practitioners working systemically in general practice. The British Association of Counselling has a division which provides a forum for those working in clinical settings, with a special interest group for those counselling in general practice.

Help for children can also be found directly through the Association of Child Psychotherapists. For anyone living near enough, the Child and Family Department of the Tavistock Clinic in London, offers not only a Youth Counselling Service, but also an Under 5's Counselling Service. A referral from a GP is preferred, but they do accept self-referrals. The Intake Secretary will also advise on local clinics and help available. Part of the work of the Clinical Service of the British Association of Psychotherapists is to offer consultation interviews to assess for treatment not only of adults, but also children and adolescents.

The Health Visitor

Other health professionals are on hand, and the health visitor is in a unique position to speak with young mothers, and the elderly, and to spot possible problems, and to liaise with the medical practice. A plan put forward by Tessa Jowell, the Minister for Public Health, is that health visitors should become 'super godparents' to young families, and their role with young families should be extended. This is part of the government's plan to ensure that children are more closely monitored on the road to adulthood. It is hoped that additional financial resources will be channelled towards children and families *before* they have reached a crisis situation. Ms Jowell says the strategy 'is not about state enforced parenting but that a gap had been identified in provision of children's services up to the age of three'. It will be a prevention service, rather than the rescue services offered at present.

Relate

One of the most common fears expressed about consulting a professional over personal anxieties is that one will be exposed and therefore more vulnerable. This is especially so if seeking help together with a partner. People are wary about what might be revealed about and to the *other* as well as about themselves. The decision to seek any kind of marital therapy does often mean a leap into the dark, where secrets may well be brought into the open, and then what? This should be seen as a new beginning, a fresh start, but only if both partners can be honest and direct. In addition, both partners have to be in agreement that change is what they want. As simple as this may sound, it comes as a surprise to some couples.

The organization Relate is probably the best known marital counselling service and it sees both couples and people individually for problems with relationships. In the year 1996/97, 386,200 interviews were given. According to Relate, anyone who rings for an appointment will be seen fairly swiftly for an initial consultation. In practice, those wanting 'out of hours' appointments often have to wait some time. If appropriate, Relate can and does help couples to find a way to separate in a manner which will lessen problems in the future.

The Phoenix Divorce Recovery

The Phoenix Divorce Recovery runs a series of seminars in London designed to help men and women after the breakup of a relationship. The founder, John Edmiston, believes that a support group combined with a series of seminars acts as a helpful new network. A feeling of 'all in the same boat' is found to be comforting and helpful.

National Council for One Parent Families

The National Council for One Parent Families has a comprehensive information manual *Getting Through* which covers all aspects of one-parent life. It is a lone parent's guide to gaining the best help and advice. The organization is committed to improving the services to all lone parents and to those who work with them. They have also published a guide to *Holidays for One-Parent Families* (March 1998) which is full of suggestions.

The Family Mediation Service

The Family Mediation Service is part of the work of the Institute of Family Therapy, and they have produced an excellent pamphlet on *Separation–Divorce: Telling your Children* and also one for children called *Is Your Family Changing? Are Your Parents Separating?* The latter explains to children why they may need to talk to an adult, an outsider, and what it would mean to see a mediator. The Mediation Service offers separating couples an opportunity to discuss issues arising from their separation together with a trained mediator. This is a non-profitmaking organization and they charge fees on a sliding scale according to income. Under the same umbrella (the Institute of Family Therapy) is the Lesbian and Gay Family Service, established in 1994. This offers a comprehensive service to lesbian and gay people and their families. As well as working on other aspects of relationships which may be causing concern, it also recognizes that homophobia can have a marked impact on people's lives. If a referral is made by a doctor, the social services or a member of the health or legal profession, the referrer will have to pay for the costs, whereas if it is a self-referral, the costs are paid by the client.

The National Association of Bereavement Services

There is a growing acceptance that counselling is effective in many situations. Bereavement counselling is one such area. After the death of someone close, some people begin to feel that the rest of the world is moving on without them, and they are left behind. After initial sympathy from family and friends the bereaved person often appreciates time spent with a trained volunteer in order to untangle some of the unresolved feelings about the person who died, and perhaps about the way he or she died. The National Association of Bereavement Services provides a very helpful leaflet, 'The Experience of Grief' and also information about organizations which will offer specific help about different areas of loss such as miscarriage, suicide or murder of a loved one.

Youth Line

This helpline has been launched by the bereavement charity CRUSE for children whose parents have died. They offer counselling and support. There are approximately 200,000 children and young people in the United Kingdom who have lost a parent.

Al-Anon and Alateen

Although most people are aware of Alcoholics Anonymous, the support given by Al-Anon to families and friends of alcoholics is invaluable. Alateen is there to help young people who have been affected by someone else's drinking, usually a parent. There are more than 1,000 Al-Anon and Alateen self-help groups in the United Kingdom and Eire.

The Lesbian and Gay Lawyers Association

The Lesbian and Gay Lawyers Association, which has 480 members, can be contacted direct by speaking to the organizer, Martin Downs, for further information. He will make a referral to a local lawyer who will act with specialist knowledge about homosexual issues.

ADDITIONAL SUPPORT FOR FAMILIES

Professionals from different backgrounds are increasingly available to provide appropriate help. More emphasis is being given to support during the early years of parenting and a wide range of advice is available. There are organizations which will provide a listening ear, using basic counselling skills and will support parents in a non-judgemental way. Someone to talk to can be especially important when a baby with a disability is born, when parents may need additional help to keep the family together.

Mencap

A Mencap survey found that 200 children are born each week in the United Kingdom with learning disabilities, and this organization is there to support the families concerned. Mencap and other charities offering help with a particular disability are available to offer parents emotional support and reassurance, and practical help in caring for their children.

Parentline

Although groups for parents under stress emerged in the 1970s, the national helpline for parents began in 1993, to provide vital support at times of crisis, particularly in relation to fear of physically harming a child. During 1996, 24,000 calls were received from parents, which were all answered by volunteers who are parents themselves. It is therefore parents supporting and listening to parents. Through Parentline mothers or fathers or anyone caring for a child can reach out for help and thus reduce their isolation. Parentline works closely with other agencies in the field of child protection and will make appropriate suggestions when a caller needs professional help. By using the helpline parents under stress can vent their anger and frustration onto another parent, and not on their children.

Parents in Partnership–Parent Infant Network

In 1994 PIPPIN was set up. Its focus is on encouraging men as well as women to provide their infants with a 'secure base' right from the start, by helping new parents to be aware of the way healthy family and parent–child relationships develop. It helps couples give thought to making a family and starts *before* a baby is born.

Exploring Parenthood

The charity Exploring Parenthood, led by a team of professionals from the child and family mental health services, consults with parents and provides programmes, in partnership with parents, about parenting. Its vision is to raise the status of parenthood in our society and to support parents *before* they are in crisis.

Full Time Mothers

This organization was founded in 1990 in the face of relentless social and economic pressures on mothers to return to work; it exists to help all parents who would like the choice of looking after their children. There are local support groups for mutual encouragement, and members write to their MPs to press issues relevant to their aims. Their campaign cry is, 'A child's need – a mother's right.'

Parents at Work

This charity promotes family friendly work-places. It campaigns not only to improve the quality of life of working parents but also to ensure that children's needs are met too. It lobbies the government for reforms and employments rights, and recommends improvements to employers, and policymakers. PAW started in 1985. It now has 1,500 parent members and 350 corporate members. A booklet, *Workplace Groups*, can be obtained from PAW.

ParentAbility

ParentAbility is a National Childbirth Trust network of disabled people who are parents, or who hope to become parents. ParentAbility also offers its services to professionals who work alongside disabled parents, and can help with training for both professional and voluntary workers. Part of their work is to campaign to improve services and support for disabled people in pregnancy. There is a practical helpline to answer questions and to provide information about equipment and adaptations. Their resource list is on hand with useful contacts and addresses for finding out about pregnancy, parenthood and disability.

Home-Start

Home-Start was launched in 1973, and was established as a charity in 1981. It is an organization in which volunteers offer regular support, friendship and practical help to young families under stress in their own homes. Lonely or isolated parents, a single parent, families with multiple births, or families with several pre-school children can all be helped. Home-Start hopes to prevent family crisis and breakdown, and emphasizes the pleasures of family life, providing a breathing space for parents and elbowroom for many professional workers who refer any family with at least one child under five to the scheme. All the volunteers attend a course of preparation before being linked with families. There are now over 200 schemes with more than 5,000 volunteers visiting families throughout the United Kingdom.

Those in the caring professions are there because they do *care;* the volunteer networks, often supported by trained professionals from either the social services or the national health service, are the first lines of defence if a family falters for any reason. These services provide a broad supportive base for families. The national organizations, usually charities, are a mine of information and advice and no one should hesitate to contact a relevant agency. There really is no need for anyone to say 'I had no one to talk to' or 'I thought there was no one who would understand what I was going through.'

12   Resources

Acceptance 64 Holmside Avenue, Sheerness, Kent ME12 3EY
   Telephone: 01795 661463
Al-Anon Family Groups UK 61 Great Dover Street, London SE1 4YF
   Telephone: 0171 403 0888
Alateen 61 Great Dover Street, London SE1 4YF
   Telephone: 0171 403 0888
Association of Child Psychotherapists 120 West Heath Road,
   London NW3 7TU *Telephone:* 0181 458 1609
Association for Shared Parenting PO Box 2000, Dudley,
   West Midlands DY1 1YZ *No telephone number available*
Both Parents Forever 39 Clonmore Avenue, Orpington, Kent,
   BR6 9LE *Telephone:* 01689 854343
Bowlby Group Sidney Sussex College, Cambridge CB2 3HU
   No telephone number available
British Association for Counselling 37a Sheep Street, Rugby,
   Warwickshire CV21 3BX *Telephone:* 01788 578328
British Association of Non-parents BM, Box 5866,
   London WC1N 3XX *No telephone number available*
British Association of Psychotherapists 37 Mapesbury Road,
   London NW2 4HJ *Telephone:* 0181 452 9823
British Confederation of Psychotherapists 37a Mapesbury Road,
   London NW2 4HJ *Telephone:* 0181 830 5173
Brook Street Pregnancy Advice for Young People
   233 Tottenham Court Road, London W1P 9AE
   Telephone: 0171 323 11522
Carers National Association 20–25 Glasshouse Yard,
   London EC1A 4JS *Telephone:* 0171 490 8818
Child Poverty Action Group 11–15 Bath Street, London EC1V 9PY
   Telephone: 0171 253 3406 *Fax:* 0171 250 0622
Childfree *Internet:* http://www.missouri.edu/-c489011
Childless by Choice *Internet* http://www.now2000.com/cbc
Childline Freepost 1111, London N1 0BL *Telephone:* 0800 1111
Children's Society Edward Rudolph House, Margery Street,
   London WC1X 0JL Telephone: 0171 837 4299
Conservative Family Institute Cranmere House, Trews Weir Reach,
   Exeter, Devon EX2 4EG

Cruse Youth Line *Telephone:* 0181 940 3131
Daycare Trust Childcare Helpline *Telephone:* 0171 405 5617
Exploring Parenthood The National Parenting Development Centre,
4 Ivory Place, 20A Treadgold Street, London W11 4BP
Telephone: 0171 221 6681
Exploring Parenthood [Advice Line] 4 Ivory Place,
20A Treadgold Street, London W11 4BP
Telephone: 0171 221 6681
Families and Friends of Lesbians and Gays [FFLAG] PO Box 153,
Manchester M60 1LP
Families Need Fathers 134 Curtain Road, London EC2A 3AR
Telephone: 0171 613 5060
Family Policies Study Centre 9 Tavistock Place, London WC1H 9SN
Telephone: 0171 388 5900
Family Services Forum *Internet:* Compuserve GO:MYFAMILY
Full Time Mothers PO Box 186, London SE3 5RF
Gingerbread Association for One Parent Families
16–17 Clerkenwell Close, London EC1R OAA
Telephone: 0171 336 8183
Gingerbread Northern Ireland 169 University Street,
Belfast BT7 1HR *Telephone:* 01232 234568
Gingerbread Scotland Maryhill Community Hall,
304 Maryhill Road, Glasgow G20 7YE
Telephone: 0141 353 0989
Grandparent Resource Center Wilmington Senior Center,
1901 N. Market Street, Wilmington, DE 19802, USA
Telephone: 00 1 651 3420
Grandparents' Federation Moot House, The Stow, Harlow, Essex
CM20 3AG *Telephone:* 01279 444964
Grandparents Forum Advice
Internet: http://www.yoyweb.com/wospace
Grandparents and Parents Support [GAPS]
Telephone: 01484 641814
Grandparents Parenting ... Again 1014 Hopper Avenue, Suite 221,
Santa Rosa, CA 95403, USA
Internet: http.//members.aol.com/GranyAnie/grg.html
Grandparent Support Organisation Brace House, 57 Lyon Street,
Newtown, Southampton, Hants SO14 0LW
Telephone: 01703 632387
GrandsPlace *Internet:* http://www.grandsplace.com
Happy Families PO Box 1060, Doncaster DN 9QE
Home-Start UK 2 Salisbury Road, Leicester LE1 7QR
Telephone: 0116 233 9955

Institute of Family Therapy 24–32 Stephenson Way,
London NW1 2HX   *Telephone:* 0171 391 9150
Kids' Clubs Network Bellerive House, 3 Muirfield Crescent,
London E14 9SZ   *Telephone:* 0171 512 2112
Fax: 0171 512 2010
Lesbian and Gay Lawyers' Association PO Box 71, Beckenham,
Kent BR3 5ZG *Telephone:* 01273 625625
Life Pregnancy Care 22 Norfolk Row, Sheffield, S1 2PA
Telephone: 0114 2758107
London Women's Clinic 113–15 Harley Street, London W1N 1DG
Telephone: 0171 487 5050
Mencap Freepost, Bristol BS38 7AH *Telephone:* 0171 454 0454
MMG – My Mums' Group incl. Lesbian Mothers,
6 Forresters Terrace, Teignmouth, Devon TQ14 3BP
Telephone: 01626 773925
National Association of Bereavement Services 20 Norton Folgate,
London E1 6DB   *Telephone/Fax:* 0171 247 0617
Telephone referrals: 0171 247 1080
National Council for One Parent Families 255 Kentish Town Road,
London NW5 2LX   *Telephone:* 0171 428 5400
National Family Mediation 9 Tavistock Place, London WC1H 9SN
Telephone: 0171 383 5993
National Foster Care Association Leonard House,
5–7 Marshalsea Road, London SE1 1EP
Telephone: 0171 828 6266
National Step Family Association Chapel House, 18 Hatton Place,
London EC1N 8RU *Telephone:* 0171 209 2460
ParentAbility Alexandra House, Oldham Terrace, Acton,
London W3 6NH   *Telephone:* 0181 992 2616
Parentline Endway House, Endway, Hadleigh, Essex SS7 2AN
Telephone: 01702 559900
Parents at Work Freepost ND 6232, London EC2B 2JE
Telephone: 0171 628 3578
Parents' Friend Stringer House, 34 Lupton Street, Hunslet, Leeds
LS10 2QW *Telephone:* 0133 2674627
Parents In Partnership – Parent Infant Network [PIPPIN]
Derwood, Tods Green, Stevenage, Herts SG1 2JE
Telephone: 01992 471355
Parents Together (affiliated to the national organization FFLAG)
PO Box 464, London SE25 4AT *Helpline:* 0181 650 5268
Phoenix Divorce Recovery *Telephone:* 0181 893 9665
Pregnancy Advice Service 11 Charlotte Street, London W1P 1HD
Telephone: 0171 637 8962

Pregnancy Care and Counselling Service (LIFE) 83 Margaret Street, London W1N 7HB *Telephone:* 0171 637 1529

Primary Health Care Trust Majestic House, High Street, Staines, Middlesex TW18 4DG *Telephone:* 01784 441782

Relate Headquarters, Little Church Street, Rugby CV21 3AP *Telephone:* 01788 5732341 (*see telephone book for local numbers*)

Samaritans Help Line 46 Marshall Street, London SW1V 1LF *Telephone:* 0345 909090

Single Parent Action Network Millpond, Baptist Street, Easton, Bristol BS5 0YJ *Telephone:* 0117 9514231 *Fax:* 0117 9355208

Solicitors Family Law Association PO Box 302, Orpington, Kent BR6 8QX *Telephone:* 01689 850227

SonFlowers *Helpline:* 01327 301344 *Fax:* 01327 301344

Stonewall 16 Clerkenwell Close, London EC1 0AA *Telephone:* 0171 336 8860

Tavistock Marital Studies Institute 120 Belsize Lane, London NW3 5BA *Telephone:* 0171 447 3723

Thinking Families Collingwood Surgery, Hawkey's Lane, North Shields, NE29 0SF *No telephone number available*

United Kingdom Council for Psychotherapists 167 Great Portland Street, London W1N 5FB *Telephone:* 0171 436 3002

WATCH? [What about the children?] 60 Bridge Street, Pershore, Worcs. WR10 1AX *Telephone:* 01386 561 635

Women's Aid Federation PO Box 391, Bristol BS99 7WS *National Helpline:* 0345 023468 *London Helpline:* 0171 392 2092

Woman's Space *Internet:* http://www.wospace.cnation.com

Young Minds 102–8 Clerkenwell Road, London EC1M 5SA *Telephone:* 0171 336 8445

Bibliography

Barnes, Gill Gorell (1984) *Working with Families.* London: Macmillan.

Barnes, Gill Gorell, Thompson, P., Daniel, G. and Burchardt, N. (1998) *Growing Up in Stepfamilies.* Oxford: Clarendon Press.

Bloom, Sandra (1998) *Creating Sanctuary.* London: Routledge.

Bowlby, John (1953) *Child Care and the Growth of Love.* Harmondsworth: Penguin Books.

Bowlby, John (1969) *Attachment and Loss*, Volume 1. London: Hogarth Press.

Bowlby, John (1973) *Separation, Anxiety and Anger.* London: Hogarth Press.

Clinton, Hillary Rodham (1996) *It Takes a Village.* New York: Simon and Schuster.

Clulow, Christopher, ed. (1993) *Rethinking Marriage.* London: Karnac Books.

Cockett, M. and Tripp, J. (1994) *Family Breakdown and Its Impact on Children.* Exeter: University of Exeter Press.

Colman, Warren (1993) 'Fidelity as a Moral Achievement' in *Rethinking Marriage.* London: Tavistock Institute of Marital Studies.

Cook, Peter (1996) *Early Child Care – Infants and Nations at Risk.* Melbourne: News Weekly Books.

Cooper, Judy and Alfillé, Helen, ed. (1998) *Assessment in Psychotherapy.* London: Karnac Books.

Curtis, Jill and Ellis, Virginia (1996) *Where's Daddy?* London: Bloomsbury.

de Toledo, Sylvie and Brown, Deborah Edler (1995) *Grandparents as Parents.* London: The Guilford Press.

Dormor, Duncan J. (1992) *The Relationship Revolution.* London: One plus One.

Family Policy Studies Centre (1997) *The Changing Face of the Family.* London: Family Policy Studies Centre.

Fleissig, A. (1991) 'Unintended Pregnancies and the Use of Contraception, Changes from 1984 to 1989'. London: *British Medical Journal* 302, 147.

Grove, Valerie (1987) *The Complete Woman.* London: Chatto and Windus.

Harlow H.F. and Zimmerman R.R. (1959) 'Affectional Responses in the Infant Monkey', *Science* 130: 421–32.

Helman, Ilse (1990) *From War Babies to Grandmothers*. London: Karnac Books.

Klein, J. (1987) *Our Need for Others*. London: Tavistock Publications.

Macdermott, Terri, Garnham, Alison and Holtermann, Sally (1998) *Real Choices for Lone Parents and Their Children*. London: Child Poverty Action Group.

Mainprice, June (1974) *Marital Interaction and Some Illnesses in Children*. London: Institute of Marital Studies, Tavistock Institute.

Martin, April (1993) *Lesbian and Gay Parenting*. London: Harper-Collins.

Robertson, J. and J. (1958) *Young Children in Hospital*. London: Tavistock.

Ruszczynski, S. (1992) 'Notes Towards a Psychoanalytic Understanding of the Couple Relationship'. *Psychoanalytic Psychotherapy* 6(1): 33–49.

Ruszczynski, S. (1993) *Psychotherapy with Couples*. London: Karnac Books.

Sacks, Chief Rabbi Dr Jonathan (1997) *The Politics of Hope*. London: Jonathan Cape.

Skynner, Robin and Cleese, John (1983) *Families and How to Survive Them*. London: Methuen.

Skynner, Robin (1995) *Family Matters*. London: Mandarin.

Switzer, S. (1995) *Child Health in the Community: A Guide to Good Practice*. London: Dept of Health.

Tomlinson, David (1990) *Luckier than Most*. London: John Curtis Books.

Trollope, Joanna (1998) *Other People's Children*. London: Bloomsbury.

Wallerstein, J. (1985) *The Long Term Effects of Divorce on Children*. New York: Basic Books.

Wallerstein, J. and Kelly, J. (1980) *Surviving the Breakup*. New York: Basic Books.

Whitfield, Professor Richard (1996) 'The Economic and Social Costs of Family Disintegration'. Rome.

Wiener, Jan, and Sher, Mannie (1998) *Psychotherapy and Counselling in Primary Health Care*. London: Macmillan.

Winnicott, D.W. (1956) 'Primary Maternal Preoccupation' in (1958) *Collected Papers*. London: Tavistock.

Winnicott, D.W. (1960) 'Ego Distortion in Terms of True and False Self' in (1979) *The Maturational Process and the Facilitating Environment*. London: Hogarth Press.

Winnicott, D.W. (1964) *The Child, the Family and the Outside World*. Harmondsworth: Penguin Books.

Winnicott, D.W. (1979) *The Maturational Process and the Facilitating Environment*. London: Hogarth Press.

Winnicott, D.W. (1992) *Through Paediatrics to Psychoanalysis*. London: Karnac Books.

Winnicott, D.W. (1993) *Talking to Parents*. Reading, Massachusetts: Addison-Wesley.

Index

Index compiled by Sue Carlton

UNHAPPY CHILDREN
Reasons and Remedies

Heather Smith

'This excellent book explores in depth why many children are unhappy...Its publication is most timely. All those with a responsibility for children - parents, teachers, youth leaders, social workers, and counsellors - need to read the whole book, if they are to benefit from it.'
Education

'Unhappy Children is immensely readable. This is the sort of psychology that ought to be absorbed by all teachers in training, and others who work with children.'
Emotional and Behavioural Difficulties: Journal of the AWCEBD

What are the situations a child might encounter when growing up that can lead to a threat to his or her emotional well being? What emotional needs are not being met? What can be done to help that child to recover a sense of well being and move on?
Remarkably free of jargon, this book presents the emotional problems of children in depth, and a variety of ways of dealing with those problems. For any professional engaged in working with children, in education, social work, medicine, or therapy, this book is an indispensable introduction to the emotional life of children with problems and how to work with them.

HELPING CHILDREN COPE WITH SEPARATION AND LOSS

Claudia Jewett

Through years of work with hundreds of bereaved children, child and family therapist Claudia Jewett has developed the simple techniques described here - techniques that any adult can use to help children through their grief. From the agonising moment when an adult must tell a child what has happened, through the shock and denial, then anger and depression, that follow. Jewett describes each stage of mourning and the behaviour that can be expected of grieving children. Using case histories and sample dialogues, she explains how to help children come to a timely resolution of their grief.